CONTOURS OF PRIVACY

CONTOURS OF PRIVACY

THE ETHNOLOGY OF A SOCIAL AND AESTHETIC CONCEPT

MARTY ROTH

ACADEMICA PRESS
BETHESDA - DUBLIN - PALO ALTO

Library of Congress Cataloging-in-Publication Data

Roth, Marty, 1934-
Contours of privacy : the ethnography of a social and aesthetic concept / Marty Roth.
pages cm
Includes bibliographical references and index.
ISBN 978-1-936320-53-0 (alk. paper)
1. Privacy. 2. Privacy--Social aspects. 3. Privacy, Right of. 4. Privacy in literature. I. Title.
BF637.P74R68 2012
302.5--dc23
2012032414

Academica Press, LLC
Box 60728
Cambridge Station
Palo Alto, CA. 94306

Website: www.academicapress.com

to order: 650-329-0685

To the new generation, Ramona, Jason and Jonas Roth

If a man passes a door which has no curtain and is not shut and looks in, he has committed no sin.

Mishkat al-Masabih.

"That's about played out, any way, the idea of sticking up a sign of 'private' and thinking you can keep the place to yourself. You can't do it–you can't keep out of the light of the Press."

Henry James, *The Reverberator*

There was a time when the affairs of all corporations were held to be as private as a man's theology is to-day. There was a time before that when his theology was held to be as public a matter as the color of his eyes. But infectious diseases, on the other hand, were once as private as the processes of a man's digestion. The history of the notion of privacy would be an entertaining tale.

Walter Lippman, "Censorship and Privacy."

Few people today would claim that their psychic life arises by spontaneous generation, independent of social conditions and environmental influences, Nevertheless, the psyche is treated as though it has an inner life of its own. This psychic life is seen as so precious and so delicate that it will wither if exposed to the harsh realities of the social world, and will flower to the extent that it is protected and isolated. Each person's self has become his principal burden: to know oneself has become an end, instead of a means through which one knows the world.

Richard Sennett, *The Fall of Public Man*

CONTENTS

PREFACE

Like its predecessor *Cultures of Memory*, this is a book made up largely of the thoughts and words of others, a gathering together of pertinent strands of discourse on the subject of privacy and its environs. I call them intellectual ethnographies. Unlike the previous book on memory this one has no fixed location in culture but shifts from place to place. The private is as much a phantom, according to Bruce Robbins, as its opposite, the public.

But a hardy phantom. To cite one of hundreds of similar statistics: according to a 1999 Wall Street Journal-NBC poll privacy was the issue that concerned Americans most about the twenty-first century (Andrejevic 2004:105). It is a subject that seems to come from nowhere: in 1890 a lone essay, "The Right to Privacy," by Samuel D. Warren and Louis Brandeis, appears and over the years receives the reverential regard and close reading appropriate to a sacred foundational document. A voluminous legal literature emerges around it and that pretty much accounts for the concept until the 1960s when social commentary and philosophical discussion begins. By this time the floodgates are open and John Hollander can correctly claim that the word "privacy" has come into "sensationally active public use in the past few decades" (5).

Whence the flood? Beate Rössler touches on the most important causes: recent interest in reconceptualizing privacy "is due to three distinct historical processes: first, the intrusion of intimacy into the public realm ["the new narcissism"] . . . secondly, radical changes in the relation between the sexes and the concomitant reconfiguration of the private sphere [feminism] . . . and thirdly, recent development in information technologies" (2005:4) The erosion of privacy alone (my last chapter) has spawned a considerable library of essays and books.

As the chapter breakdown indicates, this project is divided between the private and the forces deployed against it, primarily surveillance. The subject is also scored by a paradox: to champion privacy is to violate it. Public representation of privacy in fiction and the media violates its ostensible commitment in its frenzy to depict everything associated with this state, probing the secret corners of individual consciousness and family domesticity.

It is both contemporary and elegiac to be writing on privacy now that it has been virtually extinguished, cherished in its passing as never before. So this book is also the account of extinct species. "You already have zero privacy--get over it," a CEO announced at the launch of his company's networking software in 1999 (Glancy 1). But one must also resist the notion that prior generations lived in some paradise of reticence and respectful seclusion, safe from meddlesome officials and nosy villagers. The first rule of reading here is that everything between these covers is contested.

I began by saying that this book is filled with previous utterance, and the stress on the already written, particularly the old category of Literature, is its major date stamp: the odd old belief that that body of discourse serves particularly well as a repository of cultural attitudes. But what Literature? I can only fill the book with what I've been filled with, and I'm still that old-fashioned object, a professor (emeritus, to be sure) of nineteenth-century American Literature and film studies.

This is the second book of my retirement where I have done my best to violate the credo I absorbed in graduate school: that a book worth writing was one that made a unique contribution to scholarly or critical knowledge. This book, like the one before it, contributes little in the form of new evidence, new argument or new point of view, except, I hope, in the way of tailoring.

My primary self-criticism is that, as in the world of sports reporting, so much of the predication takes the form of strings of "saids," "states," "writes," "claims," "declares," and so on.

My thanks to Martha Roth who gave this book a hard and careful reading and belated thanks to Ed Griffin for the anecdote about the whale's heart.

1: PRIVACY AND THE PRIVATE

> Our thoughts no Commons, but Inclosures are:
> What bold Intruders then are they, who assail
> To cut their Prince's Hedge, and break his Pale?
> *Rump*

> If I should take a notion
> To jump into the ocean,
> It ain't nobody's business if I do.
> Blues lyric.

What is privacy and why does it belong to us? Is it an enclosure, an order of things? More particularly, what in the enclosure does the word "private" point to: the space enclosed, the contents of that space or the condition of untouchability that seems as if it does or should apply to those contents? Is privacy grounded? Is it a natural right or a right granted by some organizational surround--the family, the community or the state? Is it the effect of some long historical process? Or does it rather come into existence under the pressure of its own discourse? Is the corresponding desire for privacy natural or is one constructed to desire it?

Individual privacy as commonly understood features a right to be left alone ("the most comprehensive of rights and the right most valued by civilized men") and a corollary right to shield its elements (everything from data to daydreams) from exposure or theft, even from such intangible intrusions as seeing, hearing or knowing what they are (*Olmstead*). Conversely, privacy also implies the right to allow access to these privileged sites, to reveal aspects of oneself to others, as and when one chooses.

Some time around the seventeenth century, privacy was transformed from a class possession to a "universal" value and became that "natural right" that was analogous to the liberty announced by John Stuart Mill--a cornerstone of liberal democracy (232). Most modern definitions treat privacy as an essential ingredient in the production of a fully human individual or citizen. Hannah Arendt, for example, claims that privacy is valuable because it guarantees "psychological and social depth," preserving "the sacred and mysterious spaces of life" (McDougall). For her, privacy makes everything that we cherish about selfhood possible. Other writers are equally laudatory--and tautological: privacy is a fundamental value because it supports some other fundamental value, usually a constitutive feature of the self like authenticity, integrity, intimacy, etc. In their groundbreaking legal essay of 1890, Samuel Warren and Louis Brandeis saw privacy fostering a value they termed "inviolate personality" (205).[1] Ferdinand David Schoeman claims that inviolate personality nurtures individual dignity and integrity and personal uniqueness and autonomy, and Charles Fried insists that privacy "is necessarily related to and fundamental for one's development as an individual with a moral and social personality able to form intimate relationships involving respect, love, friendship and trust" (Schoeman 18 and De Cew).

These philosophical gestures underscore the absolute value, the sanctity, of selfhood and everything that belongs to it. Privacy is the condition necessary for the development of the best version of that self. When did we grant the self transcendental value? When did we erect defensive barriers around it, forbidding access to the temple unless access was granted? Writers like Bronson Alcott and Émile Durkheim took it for granted that "Individuals are sacred. The world, the state, the church, the school, all are felons whensoever they violate the sanctity of the human heart"; "The human personality is a sacred thing; one dare not violate it nor infringe its bounds" (Janna Smith and Durkheim 17).[3]

Is privacy a universal preoccupation, just modern, or just Anglo-Saxon? Maurice Cranston stated that he could find no word in ancient or medieval cultures which corresponded to the contemporary Western "privacy" (Velecky 16). "Ancient Hebrew culture lacked pervasive privacy," Steven Nock writes, " because any member's transgressions, it was believed, brought consequences from Yahweh. The Eskimos studied by Briggs lacked privacy because their economy demanded continuous cooperation" (10). Is the wide variation of what must be kept hidden reasonable? There are some societies in which people defecate in front of others; a few in which the same is true of having sex or giving birth ("Both Maria de Medici and Marie Antoinette had to give birth to their children in public"): "A king lacks nothing except the sweetness of a private life" (Brighenti 210 and La Bruyère in Elias 138). Speaking of her childhood, Sandra Cisneros said that "to be alone or to seek privacy is evil or anti-social, anti-family . . . . My family still finds my behavior rather strange" (Sanborn 1337).[4]

"Is it possible," Philippe Ariès asks, "to write a history of private life? Or does the notion 'private' refer in different periods to such different states and values that relations of continuity and difference among them cannot be established?" (1). Other questions agitating the threshold of this subject are whether or not privacy is a single category or an umbrella term for a set of overlapping terms. A federal appeals court judge described United States privacy law as like a "haystack in a hurricane"--and it is unclear whether privacy is a fundamental or secondary right (Glancy 2). Privacy, say Ariane Fennetaux and John Hollander, is an "elusive notion that is linked but not equivalent to a series of related categories" like interiority, subjectivity, intimacy and secrecy--"a word that in modern life sends pseudopodia out into the regions of other words, like 'personal,' 'intimate,' 'secret,' 'confidential,' and 'solitary,' although it never takes over any of them totally" (Fennetaux 310 and Hollander 5).

But if the self is an historical entity, there is a narrative of its constitution and shifting boundaries of privacy. A major topic here would be differences between ancient and modern privacy: Greece as against England, classical antiquity and the early modern period, and privation as opposed to positive virtue. In Greek and Roman culture privacy was understood as loss: "What one was deprived of," George Rowe writes, "included an identity and, with it, the possibility of fame. In classical thought the self is most often public, rhetorical, even theatrical--constituted by performances that must be seen and reported by others. It is also urban, competitive, and male. To be noble is to make oneself visible in the bright glare of the forum or battlefield" (310).

Rowe qualifies this generalization,

> This general tendency in the classical world to identify privacy with privation was, admittedly, only that--a general tendency. The pastoral *otium* praised in Vergil's *Eclogues,* the wry attitude toward public life typical of Horace's poetic persona, and the Stoic idealization of an essential imperviousness to the "slings and arrows of outrageous fortune" all testify in one way or another to the presence of alternative needs and attitudes So, too, do the values and beliefs of early Christians (310).

Earlier, the Epicureans had been concerned to find the means to achieve private satisfactions and a self-sufficient quiet life.

Richard Sennett expands on Rowe's footnote to Christianity, considering it a consequence of the Roman's public life becoming bloodless: "He sought in private a new focus for his emotional energies . . . . [But] this private commitment was mystic, concerned with escaping the world at large . . . . This commitment was to various Near Eastern sects, one of which gradually became dominant," i.e., Christianity (3). This religious motive lent its lustre to secular privacy and soon "the fact of being in private, alone with ourselves and with family and intimate friends . . . [became] an end in itself" (4).

Rowe continues with his little history: "Privacy began to acquire its now dominant associations with privilege, independence, and intimacy" toward the end of the sixteenth century (310). Ariès identifies early modern England as its "birthplace," referring specifically to the "popularization of diaries, letters, and autobiographies" that occurred at that time; in contemporary France, he states, there was nothing comparable (5). Ruth Yeazell dates this change two centuries later: "From the growth of suburbs and the provision of locks on inside doors to the widespread practice of silent reading, historians have identified this period [the eighteenth century] both with a newly sharpened division between the public and the private and with a newly deepened sense of the individual's interiority" (120).

There has been much speculation as to the causes of this shift: the two explanations most frequently on offer are urbanization (which anchors Yeazel's suburbs) and the Protestant Reformation. Jürgen Habermas contends that as divine authority was taken away from the church and given to the individual, the religious conscience became the "first sphere of private autonomy" (11). Other scholars have linked this "rise of the developing private self" to Protestantism's Bible reading, "its cultivation of a sense of personal sin, its search for a direct relationship with God, and its celebration of the nuclear family"; to silent prayer– "Privacie [in devotion] is to bee chosen that beeing sequestred from company, wee may more fully descend into our owne hearts, and be freer from Ostentation and Hypocrisie"; and silent reading-- "Reading to oneself, silently, already implies a certain value attached to privacy, a practice of self-communion" (Jagodzinski 1, Heywood in McKeon 42 and Brooks 29).[5] Another candidate for all of this has been "politeness": the Renaissance Humanist stress on "civility" which fostered a "desire to separate one's body and its juices from contact with other people" (Stone 171).

Mill and Benjamin Constant are often identified as the early spokesmen for modern privacy: "But neither one person, nor any number of persons, is warranted in saying to another human creature of ripe years, that he shall not do with his life for his own benefit what he chooses to do with it" [1859] ; and

> For forty years I have defended the same principle: freedom in everything . . . and by freedom I mean the triumph of the individual both over an authority that would wish to govern by despotic means and over the masses who claim the right to make a minority subservient to a majority. . . . The majority has the right to oblige the minority to respect public order, but everything which does not disturb public order, everything which is purely personal

> such as our opinions, everything which, in giving expression to opinions, does no harm to others either by provoking physical violence or opposing contrary opinions . . . all this is something individual that cannot legitimately be surrendered to the power of the state [1829] (Mill 86 and Powell).

The notion of personal privacy received extensive treatment, mainly legal, in America during the late nineteenth through mid-twentieth centuries, (arriving eventually as a plank in the United Nations' Universal Declaration of Human Rights [1948]: "No one shall be subjected to arbitrary interference with his privacy, family, home or correspondence, nor to attacks upon his honor and reputation. Everyone has the right to the protection of the law against such interference or attacks"). This process began, Deborah Nelson relates in her exciting mini-history of privacy, *Pursuing Privacy in Cold War America*, with the Warren-Brandeis essay and was extended and honed through subsequent Supreme Court decisions: "Relatively marginal in constitutional law in the half-century that followed [Warren and Brandeis], the right to privacy began to emerge in the 1950s and 1960s not only as a distinct right, but as the most fundamental right that Americans possess" (Shamir 1997:750).[6]

As defined by the two lawyers, violation of privacy was initially conceptualized as a threat to manhood: it was "patriarchal privacy" (privacy at the natural discretion of the "gentleman"); it "yoked together private property, bodily integrity, sovereignty over family members and the proprietary interest in family name." Patriarchal privacy was later replaced by "privacy of the couple" through *Griswold v Connecticut* (1965) (marital privacy trumps a state ban on contraceptives); and, after that, in *Roe v Wade* (1973), by privacy extended to the woman. Each of the court's key decisions was centered on a different site for privacy: the sanctity of the home (*Griswold*), the woman's body (*Roe*) and, later, the homosexual relationship (*Bowers v Hardwick* [1986]) (Nelson xiii, 58, 70 and 3). The U. S. Supreme Court, Nelson claims, invented the right to privacy (xv).[7]

The notion of privacy was also split between a European and an American model. James Whitman argues that

> whereas European laws on privacy have tended to emerge from ideas of a right to dignity, supported by aristocratic traditions of etiquette (including a right to control one's public image, a right to be treated as an honorable person, and a right to be protected against insult) ["right to control our public face"], American principles of privacy are more likely to be inflected by Fourth Amendment rights against State intrusion into the sanctity of the home ["right to be let alone"] (Pearson 108).

"If I may use a cosmological metaphor: American privacy law is a body caught in the gravitational orbit of liberty values, while European law is caught in the orbit of dignity. There are certainly times when the two bodies of law approach each other more or less nearly. Yet they are consistently pulled in different directions" (1163).[8]

II

In *A History of Private Life*, Ariès identifies the central aspects of modern privacy: the zoning of the body and an accompanying modesty; the valorizing of solitude; the development of a private literature of self-reflection and autobiography; the importance attached to close friendship; new ideas about the importance of daily life; and changes in the organization of living space (Brewer 7). Rössler factors the term into three: "We use the term 'private' to refer firstly to modes of action and conduct, secondly to a certain knowledge, and thirdly to spaces" (2005:6). I will also feature three meanings: a category, the *private*--the contents and products of interiority, ranging from a fleeting memory to a complete act of artistic creation; the *"privates"* (the shameful private); and *privacy*, "in private"--behavior performed with the expectation of privacy, from masturbating to a family wedding.

Interiority is usually figured as mental space filled with, among other more common properties, the peculiarities of the self: Michel de Montaigne suggested that man possessed an "*arrière boutique toute nostre* . . . . a room behind the shop which is completely our own" (Peter Burke 24). A "saturated and free interiority,"

Habermas states, is the "source of privateness" (28). These contents are "naturally" private and inaccessible to others until they have been published, when they must be protected by secondary forms of privacy--although some say that certain private matter is inexpressible (a reading of *Hamlet* for Benedetto Croce or a "language" for A. J. Ayer--a mental process, a dream, etc.) or inappropriable--one's style, *panache*, signature.

In one of his plays, J. M. Barrie presents a familiar fiction of interiority:

> [Amy] lingers among the pages [of her diary], re-reading the peculiarly delightful bit she wrote yesterday; so we could peep over her shoulder, while the reader peeps over ours. Then why don't we do it? Is it because this would be a form of eavesdropping, and that we cannot be sure our hands are clean enough to turn the pages of a young girl's thought? It cannot be that, because the novelists do it" (2).

Fiction offers us the illusion of precisely such access--instant and direct access to the interior of the self or the intimate scene (just as the privileged subject matter of contemporary television is the family). This is the foundational paradox of all representational art: the world of other people is largely closed or opaque and so we are provided, as if in compensation, with great screens which act as if they were open windows holding the secrets of the interior up for examination.[9] As Barrie noted, this is the province of the novel in particular. Milette Shamir writes that "D. A. Miller and Richard Brodhead . . . have each shown that while the creation of domestic privacy is among the conditions of the novel, and while the novel regularly reproduces an ideology of privacy, it simultaneously invades the very space it sanctifies." She exempts the American romance as a genre that respects privacy while the novel expressly violates it: "Using the example of *The House of the Seven Gables*, I will suggest, finally, that romance branches away from the novel precisely over the issue of the right to privacy: an anxiety over the potential intrusiveness of fiction and a desire to shield the domestic interior from governmental and societal policing dictate the very form of the Hawthornian romance" (1997:767-768 and 749-750).

How does one get to the interior private? Locke holds up the mental act of *reflection* as a moment when the mind can see itself at work (1975:105). Closely related to this is the process of *introspection*. René Descartes held that the mind is "fully transparent to introspection," where "Mental processes or events are supposed . . . to be played out in a private theatre [and] . . . are known directly by the person who has them either through the faculty of introspection or the 'phosphorescence' of consciousness," and his *Meditations* opens with a perfect example of this process as he descends into his personal depths, discarding from belief everything that can be doubted (Heinämaa 17 and Tanney). In introspection one drifts down or back into the interior by shutting off the active mind. The debate over whether introspection leads to accurate knowledge need not concern us here. True or false, the results of introspection or direct self-knowledge constitute the conscious interior private. Neil Rossman, however, finds such a phenomenon to be incomprehensible (52).

But is the private only conscious? Not insofar as it is a great mix of personal and common materials, Hegel declared, and Nietzsche understood further that "One's own self is well hidden from one's own self" (Villa 114 and Elliott 49). Some writers, like. Judith Butler and Louis Renza, have defined the private to include that which is beyond our self-knowledge (Butler and Renza xii).

Francis Barker (after Michael Foucault) sees modern privacy emerging in the seventeenth and eighteenth centuries when the self went indoors as part of an essential phase in the construction of the bourgeois modern world. Ironically, the concomitant phases of this process were as different from the contours of privacy as can be imagined: the mad were institutionalized; criminals were imprisoned; the poor confined to the workhouse all as part of a package deal.

Etymologically, the private is that which is separated from the rest (the Latin *privatus*). Interiority is an enclosure containing protected material (think of the enclosure system in early modern England that turned common land into private property). Barker argues that the existence of such a private place first appears in *Hamlet*, but in a "promissory form": "Hamlet asserts against the devices of the world an essential interiority . . . . a separation has already opened up between the inner reality of the subject, living itself, as 'that within that passes show,' and an inauthentic exterior: and in that opening there begins to insist, however prematurely, the figure that is to dominate and organize bourgeois culture" (Barker 52 and 35).

To the vision of early modern writers who imagined mental life "as if carried on in a totally enclosed movie theater located somewhere in the depths of the human brain," Stephen Toulmin opposes an interiority produced by internalization: our mental lives "become inner because we make them so. And we do develop inner lives, in this direct, experiential sense, because we have reasons for doing so . . . . Even the simplest of our mental tasks and procedures are at first performed overtly and publicly . . . . When, for instance, the people of Milan first saw St. Ambrose *reading to himself*, they took him for a magician" (5-6). Consciousness properly understood, Toulmin argues, we should not be prompted to divide the world into an outer and an inner, the "physical world of material things" as opposed to a "private world of inner experience" (10).

Before it received its legal guarantees, the enclosure of privacy was patrolled by affective forces with various names like reticence, modesty, honor, shame, even hypocrisy. The force of honor, here acknowledged in the breach, is attested to by Jane Austen: Anne Elliot, reading a posthumous letter of her father's, "was obliged to recollect that her seeing the letter was a violation of the laws of honor, that no one ought to be judged or to be known by such testimonies, that no private correspondence could bear the eye of others" (1998:218).

Other safeguards, like tact and discretion, are deployed after privacy has already been breached. Confidentiality, a protective glaze around certain kinds of information that passes between at least two persons, also protects privacy. Medical confidentiality dates back to the fifth century BC and the Hippocratic Oath which reads, "What I may see or hear in the course of treatment or even outside of the treatment in regard to the life of men, which on no account one must spread abroad, I will keep myself, holding such things shameful to be spoken about."

Not only does the enclosure protect its contents it also keeps things out (a little like Freud's shield against sensation). Two enclosures, the self and the house, are often equated or merged; in the Edgar Allan Poe tale, "The Fall of the House of Usher," for example, the house is a haunted mind. The historical house was "to be sheltered not merely from the competitive fray but also from the public flow of information: in Sarah Stickney Ellis's classic formulation, 'around every domestic scene there must be a strong wall of confidence, which no internal suspicion can undermine, no external enemy break through'" (Hunt 5). Shamir has written about the "recurrent metaphorical juxtaposition of the house and the human mind" in Nathaniel Hawthorne's *House of the Seven Gables*, a romance that is very much about the invasion of privacy (1997:762). In Hawthorne's *The Blithedale Romance*, Miles Coverdale thinks of his "hermitage," (his natural tree-house) as "my one exclusive possession . . . . It symbolized my individuality and aided me in keeping it inviolate" (1983:718).

It should not be surprising, then, that the history of privacy has also been written through changes in domestic architecture: "Both historians and literary critics have linked the development of subjective interiority to the increasing possibilities for domestic privacy in the early modern period. Transformation of interior space to include withdrawing chambers, private sleeping areas, and closets provided places for the new 'individual' subject to create itself" (Crane 4). These changes began in the country homes of the aristocracy between the fifteenth and early sixteenth centuries in England and filtered down to the middle class. These architectural changes were driven, according to Lawrence Stone, by a shift away from a society of kin toward a society where autonomy and privacy were respected:

> The family ceased to dine in public on high table in the great hall with the servants, and withdrew to the private dining-room. Billiard-rooms, and later smoking-rooms were built to divide the sexes. And the house was split into four basic subdivisions: the

> public rooms for mass entertaining; the family rooms; the servants' quarters with their own access staircases [back stairs, "a revolutionary invention"]; and the nursery area for the children . . . . Bedrooms were transferred upstairs, leaving the ground floor for living-quarters (Stone 4, 253-4 and 169).

Rooms were designed to have only one entrance; passage through the house was afforded by corridors. In *Aurora Floyd*, Mary Elizabeth Braddon advised gentlefolks to be careful what they said and did in front of servants: "Your servants listen at your doors, and repeat your spiteful speeches in the kitchen . . . . Nothing that is done in the parlor is lost upon these quiet, well-behaved watchers from the kitchen" (177-178).[10]

The self, however, is not always regarded as sealed. For the religious, deity is usually granted the ability to know these contents ("Almighty God, unto whom all hearts are open, all desires known, and from whom no secrets are hid"-- *The Book of Common Prayer*). Christian societies were controlled by a belief in divine watchfulness "assisted by painted icons, murals and mosaic images showing God or his son Jesus" watching (Walker 106). And from time to time various reading systems (physiognomy, phrenology, psychoanalysis) have been offered up to unlock these depths. A major trope in the fiction of Hawthorne has it that secret sin always works its way to the surface of the body, displaying itself, as in the following passage from *The Marble Faun*: "'Do you see it [guilt] written in my face, or painted in my eyes?' inquired Miriam . . . . 'Did all Rome see it, then? . . . . Or is it some blood-stain on me, or death-scent in my garments? They say that monstrous deformities sprout out of fiends, who once were lovely angels'" (1983:1025-1026). In the next chapter, I discuss a range of penetrating looks.

At the other extreme, there are contemporary intellectual drifts that would close up the space of the self and deny any private realm to the individual. In addition to splitting the self, Freud had also eliminated privacy from his world of wellness:

> The patient typically "defend[s] himself with the argument that he thought this particular story was his private business," Freud explains, hastening to add that psychoanalytical treatment "does not, *of course*, recognize any such right to asylum" . . . . That which the patient thinks he or she can cherish as "private" represents the undefeatable enemy of consciousness and narrativity (Shamir 2006:64).

If in modernity, as Walter Benjamin and others declare, one is deprived of authentic experience, then, in modernity, the contents of the private also disappear (1955:219-254). Theorists like Louis Althusser, Mikhail Bakhtin, Roland Barthes and Jean Baudrillard have vacated that realm by transforming private experience into public property since the subject is already created by ideology or linguistic codes (Baudrillard 2005). "Every time I open my mouth," Denise Riley writes, "I'm insinuating myself into some conversation which preexists me and to which my contribution is only a rustle of echoes" (2000:100).

Throughout the early modern period in Western Europe, the body became more and more private--"For the body itself is subject to a process of privatization, becoming less a subject of public discourse and open display, more a hidden object coquettishly shown and the subject of insatiable curiosity--both in regard to its parts and its movements; it was gradually deemed to be private from the neck to the ankles" (Brooks 163). The shameful private would be a dispensible category for my purposes were it not for the possibility that the private as a whole is a concept pressed out of shame, as Rachel Gurstein and Patricia Spacks assume: "I am going to argue that privacy, in its most fundamental and timeless function, serves as a social container for bodily experiences associated with shame"; "The idea of privacy always carries about it some aura of the erotic. Those 'Privacy Please' signs on the outside of a door suggest the possibility of couples at play inside the rooms they protect" (Gurstein 11 and Spacks 2003:13). Doesn't the strong feeling with which we respond to a violation of privacy--the feeling of being invaded–suggest that perhaps all expectations of privacy are held in place by shame, leading to a topic that will be up for discussion soon: "Why hide it if you're not ashamed of it?"

In 1894 a journal, the *Green Bag,* noted that rights to privacy were being extended "beyond the body of the individual to his reputation. Thoughts, emotions, and sensations have acquired legal recognition in certain respects" (Bergman 142). The private spills well beyond the self. Private things may be images or thoughts in the mind or those images or thoughts in sound-waves, on paper, canvas or in cyberspace. The condition of privacy attaches to objects that are stamped by our inwardness. Privacy ripples outward (the difference between *the private* and in private) to take in surrounding space, to include what we make, what we own (our private property), what we belong to (a family, an intimate circle, a friendship or an acquaintanceship), and, to some extent, how we live in our world and what we make of our lives–both the "good" and the "way" of Mill's phrase, "pursuing our own good in our own way" (49). "But how," Patricia Boling asks "is the idea of privacy as controlled access connected to the idea of privacy as one's ability to make decisions that critically affect one's life, such as whether to continue a pregnancy?" (21). "In private" is a status that one carries around like a shield: Flora Bell Graham was attending a county fair in Alabama in 1961. As she left the fun house air jets blew up her dress and a newspaper photographer snapped the picture. A newspaper published it and she sued. The Alabama Supreme Court held that she had a reasonable expectation of privacy even in a public place (Calvert 203-204).

The most immediate example of such a surround is the space of social encounter (or "flight distance"), a space that does not properly belong to anyone. Still, it is highly graduated in terms of access. This space, however, can be acceptably breached if the density of a room increases beyond a certain limit (i.e., on a subway). It is also possible to claim or mark your privacy through design, by branding space, like leaving a jacket on a theater seat while you get a drink in the lobby. The rules of contact and approach are historically and culturally variable; for example, in Arab cultures "one goes out of one's way to make physical contact before speaking" (Chabot). The space of social encounter is also semantic; proximity opens and closes with, for example, the approved use of *toi* or *vous*.

Some of the space of privacy is granted by custom and law; some of it is purchased; and some is just taken. Although Philippe Ariès has stated that until the seventeenth century no one was ever alone, one could thereafter have the privacy that one was clever, strong or rich enough to impose on one's surroundings, and it could be achieved simply by moving away or hiding. Early Americans thought of privacy in this physical way: if one wanted to protect it, one simply moved west, where fewer people were likely to know or care about you. James Fenimore Cooper's Natty Bumppo knows that it is time to move further west when he can smell the wood-smoke of other campfires or hear the ring of axes (75).

The move away is often a withdrawal into nature, as Thoreau writes in *Walden*: "For what reason have I this vast range and circuit . . . for my privacy, abandoned to me by men? My nearest neighbor is a mile distant, and no house is visible from any place but the hill-tops . . . . It is as solitary where I live as on the prairies" (1985:426). Ariès identified the valorizing of solitude as a touchstone of modern privacy, dating the taste for it in France to the end of the seventeenth: "People became so fond of being alone that they wished to share their solitude with a dear friend, a teacher, relative, servant or neighbor–a second self" (5). Spacks dates it later: eighteenth century thinkers still "glorified the social. Lord Shaftesbury, for example, inquires rhetorically, 'Who is there can well or long enjoy any thing, when *alone*, and abstracted perfectly, even in his very Mind and Thought, from every thing belonging to Society'" (2003:196).[11]

Solitude can also be achieved by surrounding oneself with walls, fences or screens (like Melville's Bartleby). Classical civilization had already established the home as a primary site for privacy, for what, wrote Cicero, "is more inviolable, what better defended by religion than the house of a citizen . . . This place of refuge is so sacred to all men, that to be dragged from thence is unlawful" (Robert Smith 21). And this sentiment was frequently echoed: e.g., by

William Pitt the Elder: "The poorest man may in his cottage bid defiance to the Crown. It may be frail--its roof may shake--the wind may enter--the rain may enter--but the King of England cannot enter"; or Dostoievsky's underground man: "My own apartment was my private residence, my shell, my cave, where I hid from all humanity" (Sykes 1999:83 and Dostoievsky 79). Like the home, the garden is a site of privacy, quite distinct from our inwardness even though it often becomes a metaphor for that inwardness.

Are house and garden places of privacy just because they are private property? Many articles and chapters have argued that privacy is just a metaphoric extension of the latter (see Chlopecki or Kent). But the two categories are sufficiently different, even though there is overlap between them: they are ranked and evaluated differently, i.e., "He that steals my purse steals trash, but he that filches from me my good name . . . " Private property is valued according to an external scale of value while private things have idiosyncratic or "sentimental value," and, in the case of the shameful private, are esteemed even though they have negative or ambiguous value. Warren and Brandeis insisted that the right to privacy is qualitatively different from the right of property: the "principle which protects . . . personal productions," they argued, "is in reality not the principle of private property, but that of an inviolate personality'" (205). The following examples offered by Hollander make, first, a clear distinction between privacy and private property and, then, between private *property* and *private* property: "A sense of your own privacy is not compromised by your knowledge that everyone else has an equal amount or range of it; there is no greed extending to privacy, and no striving to exceed others in its possession. This is not true of a sense of ownership of real or other property"; and

> You own a letter written by Fred to Hilda, containing an unpublished poem and an ancillary confession to some vile misdeeds. The letter--the pieces of paper--is yours and you can write on it, rewrite what is on it, wrap sandwiches with it, start a fire with it, mop up messes with it, shred it, or even burn it. But you cannot publish any of it in any form, for the language belongs

> to Fred or his estate--*not* to Hilda or hers, and certainly not to you (9 and 16).

Katherine Adams, however, would make this distinction a matter of false consciousness. By claiming the privacy value as "inviolate" Warren and Brandeis suggest that it is "an entitlement not reducible to any previously recognizable right, an entitlement requiring a new law that is 'spiritual' rather than 'material.'" Privacy discourse, thus, suppresses "the worm at its heart to promise a seamlessly unified self that exists in a space before marketization" (12 and 11).

Judith Wagner De Cew adds anonymity to solitude and sequestration as means of securing privacy.

> I'm Nobody! Who are you . . .
> Don't tell! They'd advertise–you know!
> How dreary–to be–Somebody!
> How public–like a Frog–
> To tell one's name–the livelong June–
> To an admiring Bog (Dickinson P288).

Anonymity was the condition of life in the early modern city and contributed to the construction of modern privacy. As Charles Lamb wrote to his friend Thomas Manning in 1800, "It is a great object to me to live in town, where we shall be much more *private*, and to quit a house & a neighborhood where poor Mary's disorder, so frequently recurring, has made us a sort of marked people. We can be no where private except in the midst of London" (207). Arendt disagrees: what the city really offers is the "phenomenon of loneliness. The reason for this extremity is that mass society not only destroys the public realm but the private as well, deprives men not only of their place in the world but of their private home, where they once felt sheltered against the world" (1958:59).

One can also protect privacy through instruments of anonymity like masks and disguises--and pseudonyms: "Zenobia, by the by, as I suppose you know, is merely her public name; a sort of mask in which she comes before the world, retaining all the privileges of privacy" (1983:637). But all faces are masks, or so runs a theme of social psychology. We all play at Jekyll and Hyde, with a respectable facade hiding a more shameful private self. Perhaps Spalding Gray said it best when he defined his self-presentation as honing "the well-told partial truth to deflect the raw private truth" (McLaren). Erving Goffman and others declare our social behavior to be a series of roles ("strategies and conventions of 'self-presentation,' 'self-stylization' and 'impression management'"); when we are not being observed, we inhabit a more relaxed sphere ("off-stage," "backstage") (Peter Burke 18 and Goffman). The element of acting in simply being in the world has, according to Ann Marie Stagg, increased as we have moved into the regime called neo-liberal: in the current workplace, employers are demanding that their service-sector employees "deep act, work on and change their feelings to match the display required by the labor process" (Couldry 76).

John Adams, a master of artful communication, defended lying in the service of privacy:

> The first Maxim of worldly wisdom, constant Dissimulation, may be good or evil as it is interpreted. If it means only a constant Concealment from others of our Sentiments, Actions, Desires, and Resolutions, as others have not a right to know, it is not only lawful but commendable . . . . This kind of Dissimulation is a necessary Branch of Wisdom, and so far from being immoral and unlawfull . . . is a Duty and a Virtue (Robert Smith 29).

One can buffer the self and control access to private content in even subtler ways, for example, through modulations of voice (irony and various other forms of double-tonguing) and body: "Her remark wounded me dreadfully. That's not what I'd expected. Yet, I didn't understand that she was intentionally disguising her feelings with sarcasm; that was usually the last resort of people who are timid and chaste of heart, whose souls have been coarsely and impudently invaded" (Dostoievsky 69). Conventional language also serves a masking function, although one that is generally understood by all parties to the exchange:

> If I say, "How nice to see you," you know perfectly well that this is not meant as a report of my true feelings--even if it happens to be true. I might very well say it even if you were the last person I

> wanted to see at just that moment, and that is something you know as well as I. The point of polite formulae and broad abstentions from expression is to leave a great range of potentially disruptive material unacknowledged and therefore out of play (Nagel 6).

As I mentioned at the beginning of this chapter, the private has a number of semantic relatives: the secret, the sacred, the auratic object and others. There are also overlapping categories like leisure, which share with privacy the ability to refresh the self. The private and the secret are very close if Chekhov's aphorism--"We all have our private lives, so we must have our secrets"--is to be credited (Szabados 19). In fact, Paul Christopher Johnson makes secrecy sound just like privacy: "it entails the maintenance of an interior mental world that, by virtue of its capacity to depart from the exigencies of the immediate material and social context, allows imagined and ideal worlds to grow and, at least potentially, to nourish diversity and change" (5). But, as Sissela Bok writes, "privacy need not hide; and secrecy hides far more than what is private. A private garden need not be a secret garden; a private life is rarely a secret life . . . . Why then are privacy and secrecy so often equated? In part, this is so because privacy is such a central part of what secrecy protects that it can easily be seen as the whole" (11). The distinction between the secret and the private is always a matter for negotiation: "Things once secret (e.g., abortion) are now private and things once private (wife beating) are now secret" (Nock 8).

Like the private, the sacred is precious-seeming, set apart, not to be touched, and one feels violated when its separateness is breached: "For what makes something sacred," Durkheim wrote, is that "it is the subject of a prohibition that sets it radically apart from something else, which is itself thereby made profane" (Durham). Paradoxically, the sacred is also an order of debased objects: the sacred is divided against itself (like the private) as the precious and the abject, both equally deserving of protection.

But the private *is* sacred, as much language indicates, Warren and Brandeis's "sacred precincts of privacy," for example (195). Or as Peter Brooks notes: "The 'privacies' . . . have here become 'this sacred right.' In the examples I have cited from Rousseau and other eighteenth-century novelists, 'privacies' were becoming 'sacred'" (51). In his eulogy for James Russell Lowell, Charles Eliot Norton wrote, "I cannot take my readers, however worthy of confidence they may be, within the inner circle of intimacy, of which the charm would suffer were its sanctity violated and its seclusion disturbed," and Hawthorne wrote to his wife Sophia: "I always feel as if your letters were too sacred to be read in the midst of people–and (you will smile) I never read them without first washing my hands" (Gurstein 40 and Gay 452).

Walter Benjamin's aura, a trace of divine individuality, is, like secrecy but not privacy, destroyed by publication. Although this concept is usually attributed to an object rather than a subject, it engages subjectivity. Auratic objects, for example, create zones of privacy insofar as they demand contemplation or absorption (ones relationship to the public cultural product, the object of popular culture, is the opposite, i.e., "distraction"): "Before the painting," Benjamin wrote, "the spectator can abandon himself to his associations. Before the movie frame he cannot do so" (1955:236). The bourgeois subject, is carried along by film, not absorbed, as by the illusion of the painted planes of the canvas, and, thus, no longer exists as the subject of contemplation, interiority, or privacy.

III

In "Privacy in the Decent Society," Avishai Margalit observed that "It is not that easy to say what is so great about privacy. It would be easier, I believe, to say what is bad about invasion of privacy" (255). The privacy so earnestly defined by Warren and Brandeis, Nelson notes, can only be identified as something already lost (51). For all the difficulty of defining privacy and the private, we do know that it is an order of object or event that sends up an alarm when it is breached. "Often, there appears to be no *logical* reason why a person should feel that his privacy has been invaded. It is a feeling, an emotion, just as you sense when someone is reading your newspaper over your shoulder" (John Young 3). Violations of privacy space can generate pathological reactions: "To most of us," William James wrote, "it is even unpleasant to sit down in a chair still warm from occupancy by another person's body" (439). Language (here, that of Balzac) indicates that burglary is the most frequent metaphor for this threat, rape a second:

> The true Parisian woman, indulgent to all curiosity that she can put to profit, is implacable to that which makes her lose her prestige. Such a domiciliary invasion may be called, not only . . . an attack on privacy, but a burglary, a robbery of all that is most precious . . . . A woman is quite willing to let herself be surprised half-dressed, with her hair about her shoulders . . . . but she will never allow herself to be seen "doing" her own rooms, or she loses her pariostre, --that precious SEEMING-TO-BE!.

An eighteenth-century French writer, Joseph-Michel-Antoine de Servan, likened the seal of a private letter to the hymen of a virtuous woman (Brewer 11).

Warren and Brandeis identified the crime as "wounded feelings" (198). George Bernard Shaw's Liza Doolittle resents Henry Higgins' recording of her speech because he fails to show a proper respect for her person. But the sting of invasion evaporates or reformulates as the threshold of privacy shifts, and "most moderns can no longer detect the public harm that was deplored in almost every nineteenth-century attack on exposure" (Gurstein 47).[12] On the other hand, wounded feelings are easily, perhaps too easily, deployed, claiming too much territory in their name, so that today many people feel they have a legal right not to have their feelings hurt. Finally, the invader of privacy needn't be an intrusive subject: it may be a noise or an odor.

The barriers that enclose privacy can be properly lifted only by the resident self, but is there a limit to the access that can then be granted to others? Giving away rights figures as a voluntary act at the heart of Hobbes' theory of government and as outright theft in Marx's vision of bourgeois society. Families reach into their most private depths, as it were, and publicize sacred details in the daily papers: births, wedding, deaths. By 1769 publication (of a literary work) was beginning to be talked about as self-alienation: "a work was also the objectification of a writer's self, and the commodity that changed hands when a bookseller purchased a manuscript or when a reader purchased a book was as much personality as ink and paper . . . . . Is publication—is allowing another access to one's thoughts—an implicit alienation or forfeiture of identity?" (Mark Rose and Susan Eilenberg in Bisla187-188). We live our privacy in contradictory ways within various communities of others, and there is often a dialectical rhythm to keeping it in and letting it out. Privacy should not mean shutting out the world (as "privatization" does). Arnold Simmel declares "we become what we are not only by establishing boundaries about ourselves but also by a periodic opening of these boundaries" and a "publishing" of the private (Fennetaux 310).

With publication, privacy evaporates:" I have an exceeding odd sensation," Fanny Burney wrote of her novel *Evalina*, "when I consider that it is now in the power of any and every body to read what I so carefully hoarded even from my best friends, till this last month or two; and that a work, which was so lately lodged, in all privacy, in my bureau, may now be seen by every butcher and baker, cobbler and tinker, throughout the three kingdoms." Access may still be controlled, but unselectively, for a price. The desire to control publication has led authors (Kafka, Harriet Martineau, etc.) to bind their correspondents and executors, but as James Boswell wrote of a 1773 dinner party, "the consent of nations" is against this practice. During the party conversation, Samuel Johnson had "discoursed on the subject of literary property":

> There seems, (said he,) to be in authors a stronger right of property than that by occupancy; a metaphysical right, a right, as it were, of creation, which should from its nature be perpetual; but the consent of nations is against it, and indeed reason and the interests of learning are against it; for were it to be perpetual, no book, however useful, could be universally diffused amongst mankind, should the proprietor take it into his head to restrain its circulation . . . . For the general good of the world, therefore, whatever valuable work has once been created by an author, and issued out by him,

> should be understood as no longer in his power, but as belonging to the public; at the same time the author is entitled to an adequate reward (Bisla 182).

In an ingenious reading of Wilkie Collins' *The Moonstone*, Sundeep Bisla argues that the detective novel acts out an understanding of this authorial loss of privacy after publication by suspending "publication" as long as it can: "a style of fiction asserting the author's proprietary claims for at least the length (sometimes covering a staggering number of pages and individual serial parts) of the narrative's duration . . . . Any and every mystery holds off the devastations wrought by publication for the longest possible time, usually almost the full length of the narrative, while still allowing the author to enjoy the benefits of being known as the creator of that text" (179 and 193) .

But philosophers like Wittgenstein and Arendt claim that the "private" is not real until it is published: "Compared with the reality which comes from being seen and heard, even the greatest forces of intimate life–the passions of the heart, the thoughts of the mind, the delights of the senses–lead an uncertain, shadowy kind of existence unless and until they are transformed, deprivatized and deindividualized, as it were, into a shape to fit them for public appearance" (Arendt 1958:50). In the case of fiction, memoir and autobiography, publication highlights another problem, that one's own privacy is intimately tied up with the privacy of others. Who owns your life story? This question was raised by a lawsuit brought by original cast members of the musical *A Chorus Line* convinced that producer Michael Bennett had "insufficiently remunerated them for a script built on their oral histories of childhood abuse, marital woes, and professional struggles" (Apter 91).

Invasions of privacy, that "surging outer world that threatened the peace of the home," come in two waves, the "front-door" invasion of the state and the "backdoor" invasion of community and media curiosity: In Dickens' *Pickwick Papers* Bagnet Pott, the editor of the *Eatanswill Gazette,* tells Mr. Pickwick, "But I trust, sir . . . that I have never abused the enormous power I wield. I trust, sir, that I have never pointed the noble instrument which is placed in my hands, against the sacred bosom of private life, or the tender breast of individual reputation" (Chase 7 and Dickens 162). But Hetta Carbury of Anthony Trollope's *The Way We Live Now* "had heard that everything was put into newspapers in America" (740).

> Even as it was defining itself as a private sphere, then, the middle-class home was subject to invasion on two fronts: the front-door intrusion by official authorities and institutions, forever suspecting the privacy of the house to be a cover-up for potential fragmentation; and the back-door intrusion by the "masses," who regarded the very invasion of that sphere a mode of exercising power, especially through exposing hidden depravity carefully concealed in the middle-class home (Shamir 1997:757).

Early travelers to the United States were impressed by the curiosity of the inhabitants, perhaps a consequence of the "severely intrusive nature of Puritan society," perhaps a condition of geography. "On arriving amongst the Americans," wrote Isaac Weld, "a stranger must tell where he came from, where he is going, what his name is, what his business is; and until he gratifies their curiosity on these points and many others of equal importance, he is never suffered to remain quiet for a moment." And Henry Adams later commented: "Almost every writer spoke with annoyance of the inquisitorial habits of New England and the impertinence of the American" (Robert Smith 35 and 36).

The second of these invasions was one of Henry James' great themes. "One sketches one's age imperfectly if one doesn't touch on that particular matter: the invasion, the impudence, the shamelessness of the newspaper and the interviewer, the devouring publicity of life, the extinction of all sense between public and private." In the notebook entry outlining the story of *The Bostonians*, he fulminates against "the vulgarity and hideousness of . . . the impudent invasion of privacy" (1987:40 and 19). His novella *The Reverberator* contrasts two families, the Proberts and the Dossons: the first "are profoundly distraught at having become an object of public attention . . . . They experience a sense of 'excrutiation–of pollution.' The Dossons, on the other hand, are completely mystified and bewildered by the Probert's aversion to, and phobia against, public exposure" (Schoeman 12).

The reporter in the James novella

> [wants to publish] the most universal society-paper the world has seen. That's where the future lies, and the man who sees it first is the man who'll make his pile. It's a field for enlightened enterprise that hasn't yet begun to be worked. The society news of every quarter of the globe . . . from day to day and from hour to hour and served up at every breakfast-table in the United States . . . . I'm going for the secrets, the *chronique intime*, as they say here; what the people want is just what isn't told (60-61).

Former President Ulysses S. Grant, as he lay dying of throat cancer, was subjected to news reports revealing "all his private, personal habits, as to the neatness or lack of it, capping the whole business with a minute description of the state of his teeth, the accumulation of tartar upon them, and the neglect of his toothbrush" (Robert Smith 119).

It was not only the media; representations of all kinds were testing the fragile boundaries between public and private. Anthony John Harding has written of a watershed moment in English literature around 1800 when biography turns from a respectful to an invasive genre as it moves between emulation of heroism and the pleasure of revealing dirty secrets. Writing in response to James Currie's life of Robert Burns in 1816, Wordsworth could still say

> The life of Johnson by Boswell had broken through many pre-existing delicacies, and afforded the British public an opportunity of acquiring experience, which before it had happily wanted . . . . you will probably agree with me in opinion that biography, though differing in some essentials from works of fiction, is nevertheless, like them, an art—an art, the laws of which are determined by the imperfections of our nature, and the constitution of society. Truth is not here, as in the sciences, and in natural philosophy, to be sought without scruple, and promulgated for its own sake, upon the mere chance of its being serviceable; but only for obviously justifying purposes, moral or intellectual.

IV

> And it was a worthy remark of Julius Drusus to the workmen who offered, for three thousand crowns, to arrange his house so that his neighbors would no longer be able to look into it as they could before. "I will give you six thousand," he said; "to make it so that everyone can see in from all sides." The practice of Agesilaus is noted with honor, of taking lodging in the churches when traveling, so that the people and the gods themselves might see into his private actions (Montaigne 613-614).

The relative weight of state privacy and publicity has been frequently debated, and Immanuel Kant once insisted that everything about government should be open. His transcendental principle of the publicity of public law stipulated that "All actions that affect the rights of other human beings, the maxims of which are incompatible with publicity, are unjust" (104). According to Foucault, "the Rousseauist dream that motivated many of the revolutionaries . . . . was the dream of a transparent society, visible and legible in each of its parts, the dream of there no longer existing any zones of darkness" (1980:152). A similar ideal has been proposed for the individual: "As Meister Eckhart said, we call him a good man who reveals himself to others and, in so doing, is of use to them . . . . Thus Sartre held that 'transparency must substitute itself at all times for secrecy'" (Bok 17).

The right to privacy is often seen to be in conflict with other rights–with freedom of speech or the right of the press to produce an informed electorate, but mainly with the public good (too often an illusory national security, the "sacred" of the state). This is the subject of Amitai Etzioni's *The Limits of Privacy*, which explores whether and when "we are justified in implementing measures that diminish privacy in the service of the common good" (3). The areas he explores include the violation of the privacy of mothers by HIV testing of their newborn children; Megan's Laws, which attempt to protect children from repeat sex offenders; phone-tapping of the Internet by government; the development of a powerful biometric ID system; and the lack of privacy of medical records.

But actual states (and individuals) do not agree with Kant and go well beyond the threshold of only keeping secrets when not doing so would defeat the purpose of a project. The doctrine of *arcana imperii* asserted the monarch's right to withhold secrets of state from public scrutiny. According to the terms of the Vienna Convention on Diplomatic Relations (1961), to which almost every country in the world subscribes, diplomats meeting in private, or communicating with their ministries, may rely absolutely on secrecy. If they suspect publication, it is feared, the whole machinery of international diplomacy will break down. This was the issue raised during the 2011-2012 Wikileaks/Assange/Manning episode: "Is the publishing of confidential U. S. state documents an act in support of the freedom of information, of the people's right to know, or is it a terrorist act that poses a threat to stable international relations?" (Zizek). The government claimed the latter, an example, Slavoj Zizek writes, of the doctrine of the "necessary lie" that conservative philosopher Leo Strauss identified as the glue that holds democracy together.[13]

The specter of national security leads to conundrum and paradox; secrecy multiplies absurdly: there are cases "in which disclosing the exact reason why access to a document is denied would unavoidably entail the disclosure of the document's very content . . . . Along the same lines, an authority could even refuse to deny or confirm *the very existence* of the requested document--which is known in US law as a Glomar response" (Gosseries). As Scott Michaelson writes, "it is something best acknowledged by being unacknowledged, and best considered by not being considered," so that, for example, the man who was hired by Lincoln to spy on the Confederacy and then sued the government because he wasn't paid had his claim disallowed because to sue was to retrospectively breach the contract (134-135). National security poses, as K. A. Taipale says, a "wicked problem":

> Security and privacy are not a balancing act but rather dual obligations of a liberal democracy that present a *wicked problem* for policy makers. Wicked problems are well known in public policy and are generally problems with no *correct* solution. Wicked problems reveal additional

> complexity with each attempt at resolution and have infinite potential outcomes and no *stopping rule*--that is, the process ends when you run out of resources not when you reach the correct solution (127).

The negative form of the transparency argument is the charge that only people who have done something they want to hide demand privacy–a return to the condition of privacy until its turn in the eighteenth century. Consider Georgianna Ziegler's collection of early modern phrases for privacy, which includes items like a "closet of villainous secrets" and a "brewing place of poisons" (85 and 86). And this charge seems most congenial to democracy, as Godkin wrote in 1927: "In all democratic societies today, the public is disposed either to resent attempts at privacy, either of mind or body, or to turn them into ridicule" (Gurstein 56).

In *Philosophical Dimensions of Privacy*, Schoeman asks if privacy is good for one? In support of the negative he observes that it creates an atmosphere "in which both deceit and hypocrisy may flourish"; that the "right to privacy often stands in the way of vigorous public debate on issues of moral significance"; and that it raises the possibility that privacy increases "human vulnerability through increased sensitivity to shame and embarrassment" (1 and 6). Privacy thus points in opposite directions: it is a value that allows us freedom from control and the freedom to be ourselves and be intimate with others, and it is also a cloak behind which we can hide various faults. From a religious perspective, privacy is generally a negative value, the mark of our fallen state, a painful but necessary condition of earthly life--as expressed in the poem "Gnosis," by Christopher Cranch:

> We are spirits clad in veils;
> Man by man was never seen;
> All our deep communing fails
> To remove the shadowy screen.

The preceding investigation into the nature and extent of privacy, however, is moot because privacy has been exposed as a commodity service that protects only those who have the money or power to afford it: "Privacy is an object of exchange. It is bought and sold in hospitals, transportation facilities, hotels, theaters, and, most conspicuously, in public restrooms" (Schwartz 743). Nancy Cott points out how privacy rides on ideological fault lines: "The actual attainment of privacy . . . has become relinked to privilege--economic privilege--since those who are poor . . . are most pervaded by public oversight," single mothers, for example (542). The power deployed is not merely economic, but normative: in *Bowers v. Hardwick*, which denied privacy of the bedroom to homosexuals, "the right to privacy has been formed around a . . . normative version of a two-parent heterosexual marriage and family life," and Iris Marion Young points out in respect to "personal space" that the elderly and infirm do not have a home to be private in at all (Cott 542 and Goodall 194). "The defense of privacy," Katherine Adams concludes, " should be read alongside other strategies for consolidating white, male, and capitalist privilege such as antisuffragism, lynching, Jim Crow, segregation, nativism and laissez-faire defenses of property and market liberalism" (10). Sean Cubitt widens the historical lens: "Privacy was only ever the privilege of a small proportion of the world's population for a brief period in history. For about 150 years, the European bourgeoisie enjoyed private rooms, private water closets and a life distinct from the life of the street. That period is now over."

2. THE PRIVATE AND THE PUBLIC

> Behind every man's external life which he leads in company, there is another one which he leads alone, and which he carries with him apart. We see but one aspect of our neighbour, as we see but one side of the moon.
>
> Walter Bagehot

One of the things that private points to is the quieter, darker, female half of a world divided in two: "With the advance of civilization," Norbert Elias wrote, "the lives of human beings are increasingly split between an intimate and a public sphere, between secret and public behavior. And this split is taken so much for granted, becomes so compulsive a habit, that it is hardly perceived in consciousness" (190). Many other substances, binaries and qualities are divided along this primary axis: male and female, heterosexual and homosexual, light and dark, cold and warm; politics as a public, art as a private matter.

There is controversy about how old this division is, whether it stretches back to classical antiquity or whether it too is a product of the early modern period. The history of the distinction follows the contours of the history of privacy. Two critical moments in this history might be the shrinking of privacy in the late nineteenth century under the assault of burgeoning technology and the expansion of national security following 9/11.

An early version of this division can be found in Aristotle's distinction between a public world of political activity and an opposite sphere associated with family and domestic life--the *polis* and the *oikos*--as previously noted by Werner Jaeger and Hannah Arendt. Jaeger wrote that the Greeks differentiated between the natural associations centred on the home and the political association of the city-state, in which man received "besides his private life a sort of second life, his *bios politikos*" (in Arendt 1958:24). According to Arendt, the Greek contrast between private and public was between a sphere "where the necessities of life, of individual survival as well as of the continuity of the species, were taken care of and guaranteed" ("hence [it was the realm of] women, children and slaves") and a sphere of freedom (Arendt 1958:45 and McKeon 7). As such, the private sphere was the lesser place, the place of privation.

These two categories may be little more than archaic formations, "legacies of a Victorian fantasy that the world can be divided into a controllable space (the private-affective) and an uncontrollable one (the public-instrumental)," but Jean Elshtain and Leonore Davidoff insist that they are really "inescapable terms" (Berlant 283 and Elshtain 360). As commonly used, the distinction tends to be so rigid that it amounts to an opposition, so that "the traditional and tacit habit of distinguishing between the public and the private gradually becomes concentrated into an explicit motive to separate them" (McKeon 323).[1]

Davidoff writes that these two realms have "become a basic part of the way our whole social and psychic worlds are ordered," but it is an order that is constantly shifting, "being made and remade" (228). The dividing line between public and private is inherently unstable so that there is transformation and exchange between the two. When one crosses it deep changes can occur. One can cross this border by running for public office or, on the other hand, by holding up a "filling station. From that moment you are very much in public life, and the investigating police are in no way restricted by your former right of privacy, for you have voluntarily surrendered it" (Gerald Johnson 450). The public sphere is not simply a place a private person enters unchanged; it is, Thomas Keenan writes, the "unavoidable entrance of alterity into the everyday life of the 'one' who would be human" (133).

As for exchange, Sennett tells us that the much vaunted autonomy of privacy is a public construction as well:

> . . . by the middle of the last century, experience gained in the company of strangers came to seem a matter of urgent necessity in the formation of one's personality. One's personal strengths might not develop if one did not expose oneself to strangers . . . . In the child-rearing manuals . . . of the 1870s and 1880s, we encounter again and again the contradictory themes of avoidance of worldly perils in the company of strangers and the command to learn so thoroughly . . . these hidden temptations" (24).

And contributors to the volume *Going Public* point out how, in Soviet bloc societies, the relations between the two spheres became reversed so that "People loafed in official jobs, but on their private plots practiced extremes of overwork" and "Political discussions were conducted around the kitchen table, the home represented the only place for open discussion like this; it was here rather than in any public sphere that the possibility for transcendence occurred" (Gal 271 and Nikolchina 369). Public and private exist, says David Bromwich, in "constant mutual dependency and tension" (b.1).[2]

Also, this territory is carved up in too many different ways from very different angles of approach. In an essay that covers the topic well, Jeff Weintraub distinguishes the "public sphere" discussions of Habermas from the "public life" investigations of Ariès. The public/private distinction, he says, is used to establish the boundary of the political and to demarcate "other important boundaries: between the 'private' worlds of intimacy and the family and the 'public' world of sociability or the market economy." Private and public may refer to "What is hidden or withdrawn versus what is open, revealed or accessible . . . . [and] what is individual . . . vs what is collective." "The public/private distinction, in short, is not unitary, but protean. It comprises, not a single paired opposition, but a complex family of them" (2 and 5).[3]

At various moments of social upheaval, the private becomes the new public, as in the feminist slogan "the personal is the political" or the "outing" of gay sexuality: "Lesbian and gay political and social life in the past quarter of a century has been built on making sexual identities public, arguing that ours is a political and social status; since everyone is implicated in oppressing us" (Gamson 200).[4] The dividing line is continually breached by marginal voices from the interior which make the hitherto private a matter of public consumption and discussion, as for example, when writers like Mary McCarthy or Kate Millet publish accounts of diaphragms in the 1960s (Nancy Miller 176 and 189). Conversely, when books (or television) come(s) into the home, according to Cecile Jagodzinski, public events became private concerns as well: "they could change the *mentalité*, the way of observing the self and the world, of the early modern English citizen" (22). Rössler has noted the opposing currents of privatization and deprivatization (modernization or nationalization) in history (2004:3).[5]

Roland Barthes claimed that the great irruption of the private into the public followed from the invention of the miniature camera, "or rather into the creation of a new social value, which is the publicity of the private" (1981:98). It was such a traumatic excess of the private made public that launched the privacy project in the first place: the Warren and Brandeis essay was a response to the invention of the "snap camera" by the Eastman Kodak Company in 1884--what Walter Benjamin called "the dynamite of the tenth of a second"--which meant that photographs could now be taken without the permission or even knowledge of the people involved (Villa 175 and Benjamin 1955:236). Samuel Warren had himself been the subject of media intrusion at his daughter's wedding.

The intrusiveness of photography was a major concern of genteel critics during the nineteenth and early twentieth centuries, dating back, I suppose to the moment in *The House of the Seven Gables* when the photographer Holgrave takes a photograph of the dead Judge Pyncheon which is paired with a sadistic chapter in which the narrator teases and badgers the dead judge, urging him to get up and attend to business and not fritter his time away (1983:501-512 and 583-595). In this romance, photography is identified as the form that the traditional evil eye takes in the age of technology, and this is an ironic fulfilment of Hawthorne's opening wish that the old Gothic machinery might one day be justified by modern technology. This trope plays through the tradition of investigative photojournalism from Jacob Riis to James Agee. Often the morality is reversed as in *Let Us Now Praise Famous Men* where "Agee moves from the Alabama countryside to the exterior of the house–and then, as if he is holding a camera before him as he proceeds, he penetrates into the interior, describing more and more closely: he makes his way to the 'shrine,' the 'altar,' and finally to the 'tabernacle' of the house": "Evans and Agee were respectful–one might even say awestruck–when they entered these families' bedrooms . . . . The pictures reveal a sense of the sacramental, of the purity of the modesty of these people's intimate lives" (Wydeven 108 and Sandra Phillips 21). Here again we meet, either earnestly or disingenuously, the paradox of being unable to cherish and uphold the privacy (of the poor) without exposing and profaning it.

Given all this, Cott wonders "whether the divide between the two spheres, which has always been as much ideological as descriptive"--"a feature of a particular form of social organization associated with the rise of the family, private property, and the state, as Frederick Engels argued, and also with colonialism, as Marxist and postcolonial feminist scholars insist"--"has strutted its part on the historical stage and should be retired?" (542).

For much of its history, the public sphere was the valorized pole—

> . . . that grounded maxim
> So rife and celebrated in the mouths
> Of wisest men: that to the public good
> Private respects must yield–

but in a gradual turnabout the private came to be considered the more important and authentic half (ll. 865-868). A more positive valuation of privacy began to emerge by the late eighteenth century: "It combined withdrawal from the world with privileged status . . . . Privacy and the domestic arena to which it was now presumed to attach were positively valued as an alternative to the glare, the competition, the soul-destroying machinations of public life" (Cott 541).[6] Ralph Waldo Emerson associated this value with the British, for "never nation built their party-walls so thick, or their garden-fences so high . . . . In Alfred, in the Northmen, one may read the genius of the English society, namely, that private life is the place of honor. Glory, a career, and ambition, words familiar to the longitude of Paris, are seldom heard in English speech" (1994:72 and 79).

Because of this re-evaluation, the private sphere became a protected, ultimately a "sacred," locale: American jurisprudence built protective walls around it through various Supreme Court decisions, determining that there is "a private realm of family life which the state cannot enter" (Cott 542). Privacy was valorized as the sphere where one could be or find oneself or grow, expand and mature into the best version of oneself. Under the prompting of this new dyad, the home was physically separated from the workplace: "'Gates, drives, hedges and walls around house and garden' were physical reminders of the desire for privacy" (Gan 5). For those who could afford it, this segregation was effected by a move into the suburbs.[7]

Unlike privacy, the private sphere belongs to the family not the individual, and it was imagined to be threatened by three agencies: the state, the market, and a vast surge of curiosity ranging from neighborhood gossip to the mass media. Families have their own private reserves: secrets about homosexuality, adultery, divorce, mental health, crime, sexual behavior, alcoholism; or simple secrets about personality conflicts, death, religion, academic performance and physical health problems ("Family Secrets").

Much that is private in the home passes under the name of intimacy or familiarity, both of them terms that cohabit with privacy--being private with other people-- (as well as sexual pleasure). By the middle of the nineteenth century, the Western middle classes were absorbed in a culture of family intimacy to be replaced a century later by the intimate marriage. Individuals in these units, it was imagined, felt affectionate bonds for one another. For Arendt, intimacy was a modern Western phenomenon, and she dates its "discovery" to Rousseau–the "first articulate explorer and to an extent even theorist of intimacy'" (1958:38-39).

Intimacy, according to Margalit, "means that the gaze of those who belong, with us, to the home . . . is not supposed to make us feel ill at ease" (258). The breaching of intimacy is usually felt to be extremely invasive: having our affectionate interchanges of whatever magnitude witnessed by outsiders shrivels them. ". . . sex is inherently private," Richard Mohr contends; it "creates its own inter-personal sanctuary which in turn is necessary for its success. The whole process and nature of sex is interrupted and destroyed if penetrated by the glance of an intruder."[8]

What exactly is the relationship between the cousins, privacy and intimacy, Shamir asks? "Are they interchangeable, as some have suggested, or at least interdependent, the one constituting a prerequisite for the other? . . . As Charles Fried imagines it, 'privacy creates the moral capital which we spend in friendship and love'" (2006:209). But intimacy can also destroy privacy: "the housewife wants privacy specifically to get away from her family for a time, and from her family responsibilities" (Spacks 2003:1). And intimacy, as construed by Robert Gerstein, means precisely the loss of our selves: "An experience of intimacy is first of all an experience of a relationship in which we are deeply engrossed. It is an experience so intense that it wholly shapes our consciousness and action. We do not understand ourselves to be choosing to do this or that, or to be looking here or there as we choose. Rather, whatever we do, whatever we see, is a product of the experience in which we are taking part" (76-77).

As the metaphor of the sphere suggests, private and public are usually thought of as spaces first and then as ways of being or behaving. The spatial and architectural divisions are many: workplace and home; and then divisions in the home--parlor and study ("'the first truly private space [in the private house] was the man's study' . . . this masculine enclave helped consolidate man's power over the household because it functioned as a storage space for the family secrets . . . . The study was indeed the birthplace of the liberal individual, and his most cherished sanctum") and bedrooms and bathrooms--and liminal places that negotiate between public and private, like doors and windows: "The picture window works two ways: it turns the outside world into an image to be consumed by those inside the house, but it also displays the image of the interior to the outside world . . . . In the same way that we meticulously construct our family history with snapshots, equally skillfully we represent our domesticity through the picture window"; "Windows are made to be open," Florence Nightingale wrote, "doors are made to be shut" (Shamir 2006:45, Colomina 8, and Chase 143).

"The late nineteenth century discovery of bacteria and other germs reinforced the dangerous image of public space by 'infecting' these places with permanent impurity and fear of contamination . . . . Later, in reaction to the contamination of public places, all 'hygienic' practices from washing to bathing had to be performed in the home. The domestic space was proclaimed to be the only safe and clean environment" (Cieraad 8). Warfare fails to respect the distinction between public and private space or deliberately violates it. On the other hand, groups can retain their intimate character in public places like parks or beaches. Public space can easily take an intimate stamp, as when I'm sitting with a friend in a café.[9]

There are also two selves to go with the larger division. Like the private sphere, the private self eventually triumphed: "In time, the persona one assumed in private life came to be seen as the 'real' self and public authority was less often equated with personal authenticity" (Jagodzinski 4). Sennett's *Fall of Public Man* is an account of the historical fall of the public self, that product of the conventions that once regulated relations.

> These conventions, now condemned as constricting, artificial and deadening to emotional spontaneity, formerly established civilized

> boundaries between people, set limits to the public display of feeling and promoted cosmopolitanism and civility. The romantic cult of sincerity and authenticity tore away the masks that people once had worn in public and eroded the boundary between public and private . . .

Sincerity eroded the boundary because public display was now only read as a sign of the hidden private. Public life thus lost its edge and its color: "Between 1500 and 1800," Ariès adds, "histrionic demonstrations gave way to discreet, understated gestures. People no longer attempted to cut a figure, to create an appearance, to assert themselves, they behaved properly in order to discourage attention, to pass almost unnoticed" (5). Sennett's archaic model proceeds from a dark vision of the private self, "because every self is in some measure a cabinet of horrors, civilized relations between selves can only proceed to the extent that nasty little secrets of desire, greed, envy are kept locked up" (5).[10]

> "The work of the participants [in the conference 'Feminism and the Shifting Boundaries of Public and Private'] repeatedly stressed the uneven, wavering, mutable quality of . . . [the boundary between public and private] and the uncanny power that the binary public/private has to make things of interest simply disappear" (Rooney 333).

Towering over the instabilities between the public and the private is a critique of the distinction itself--launched primarily by feminists. In Frank Capra's *It Happened One Night*, Ellie (Claudette Colbert) tells her seatmate Peter (Clark Gable), "I want to be left alone. Can't you understand English?. Please keep out of my affairs," and he replies, "Why you ungrateful brat." Patriarchy overrides privacy: a woman traveling on a public conveyance, a bus, for example, has lost her right to privacy. But she never had it to begin with; for most of its history the private sphere had little room for the privacy of most of its inhabitants. This was partially true even for men other than the master/husband, much more true for women and children. The spheres are gendered and women were restricted to the private, both by the force of (male) propriety and by reinforcing pathologies like agoraphobia. Woman, Richard Brodhead writes, was constructed as a "creature of private space, native of that separate nonpublic, nonproductive zone marked off in nineteenth-century ideology as the home or woman's sphere" (274).

Traditionally, women were allowed little space or opportunity within "their" sphere for privacy (or even safety); Nightingale wrote that "Women never have an half-hour in all their lives (excepting before or after anybody is up in the house) that they can call their own, without fear of offending or of hurting someone" (Gan 24). According to Charlotte Perkins Gilman, "such privacy as we have at home is family privacy, an aggregate privacy, and this does not insure–indeed, it prevents–individual privacy" (Shamir 2006:41).

Until quite recently, the private sphere (the vaunted home as castle) was regarded as a realm outside the law and no authority could interfere with the dynamics of domestic abuse that occurred within it. The privacy distinction, Catherine McKinnon claims, "is an ideological division that covers up male power [and] . . . lies about women's shared experience" (194). "Many feminists," DeCew writes, "worry about the darker side of privacy, and the use of privacy as a shield to cover up domination, degradation and abuse of women and others." The gothic fiction produced in England and America in the late eighteenth and early nineteenth century was largely devoted to the image of the woman, unsettled, threatened, stalked in her own home.

So where did women find their privacy? If there was no space in the home available for such a purpose, they at least had the privacy of their pockets. Ariane Fennetaux argues that few women could afford a separate room or a locked writing desk, "Yet, from the end of the seventeenth century, every woman, regardless of her rank or status, had one of several pairs of tie-on pockets, which were detachable items of clothing rather like bags worn under a woman's skirt . . . . In Richardson's novel, Pamela, who is closely watched by Mr B., uses her pocket to hide all her writing equipment . . . . 'above forty sheets of paper, and a dozen pens, and a little phial of ink, which last I wrapped in paper and put in my pocket, and some wax and wafers'" (307-308 and 323).

Beyond that, they struggled like Virginia Woolf for space within the house or garden. Ironically, the privacy that was unavailable in the home could often be carved out in public, in the streets or, later, in the automobile. Woolf even implied that the city liberated the hidden sides of the female; the inner life, unhampered by the roles of wife and mother, is let out for an airing, as in Dorothy Richardson's "Tryst": "Approaching the house, she found herself longing for a little extra time. Time to dispose of her elastically expanded being, to reassemble the faculties demanded by the coming enclosure" (Gan 59 and 104-5).

Still, for the public record, the private sphere of women was represented as a nostalgic idyll known as domesticity, and this sweet sphere has often been contrasted with another major component of the private sphere, the marketplace, seen as even more of a threat to the sanctity of the home than government. Arendt finds it ironic that property and wealth are put under the heading of the private when they have been historically of greater relevance to the public realm than any other private matter or concern and have figured, at least formally, as the chief condition for admission to the public realm (1958:58-67).

Habermas envisioned the intimate sphere as existing outside of economic determinism, "as persons capable of entering into 'purely human' relations with one another" (48). Gillian Brown finds this imaginary claim to be ironically embodied in the pathologies of agoraphobia and anorexia–conditions in which complete separation from the demands and supplies of the world is achieved--both fastened upon women (170-195).

The home had been the original marketplace, but as "both property and production relocated outside of the home personal life and family came to seem the natural locations of autonomous and authentic selfhood, imagined as both separate from and prior to economic and political activity" (Adams 11). The family was then seen to consist of a romantic couple and an "economically useless but emotionally 'priceless child'" (Weintraub 21).

Warren and Brandeis's "inviolate personality" was defined by resistance to market forces, but even after the home could no longer be seen as a site of production it was deeply involved in economic relations as a site of consumption: home began to "seem more like an incomplete collection of commodities than a refuge from the outside world" (Thomas 85 and Gallagher). Another example of the representational paradox enacted by public and private is "the extent to which domestic life itself was impelled toward acts of exposure and display"; the idyll of domesticity was largely a product of the nineteenth- and twentieth-century advertising industries through advertisements conveying the attractions of domesticity,

> mainly by placing private life on display, flooding American culture with images of intimacy, and turning previously unmentionable topics such as ladies' underwear and male impotence into subjects of social discourse . . . . At the same time, the commercialization of the private realm [by telephone, radio, television, Internet] made the notion of the home as a haven increasingly hard to sustain . . . . [filling the home] with anxiety-inducing messages about the need for additional spending (Chase 7 and Gallagher).

Although it has changed its valence, the private sphere has had relatively stable boundaries until modern times, but its opposite, the public sphere, didn't even exist until the eighteenth century, according to Habermas. It was certainly not the space of court or church or bourse culture, the spheres of "Public Authority," the inauthentic public spheres, which were put on alert by the new true public sphere.

> Habermas's account involves three separate but sometimes overlapping spheres. The first is that of public authority and the state, what in the eighteenth century was often referred to as "police"; but which also includes the realm of the court; the second is the [bourgeois] "pubic sphere" of politics and letters centred on "the town"; and the third is the private sphere which, in turn, divides into the world of commodity exchange and social labour, on the one hand, and the family's internal space, what is sometimes termed the "intimate sphere," on the other (Brewer 4).

The bourgeois public sphere may be conceived above all as the "sphere of private people come together as a public" (Habermas 27). Habermas's public sphere came into existence at the end of the seventeenth century with the creation of a press that addressed all possible participants in the belief "that private individuals can arrive at a rational consensus about the justice of claims upon shared resources" (Pauline Johnson 11). Its characteristics include universal access and rational debate.

This public sphere is urban; it is also constituted by certain kinds of space in which the participants can assemble: "embodied in a number of institutions, most notably the clubs, salons, coffee-house coteries and tavern societies that flourished with such abundance in European polite society" (Brewer 3). As Stallybrass and White have suggested, an important part of the creation of this "public sphere" was the cleaning up and reconceptualization of urban space. Serial periodicals largely worked this change: Addison and Steele were responsible for the "creation of a sublimated public body without smells, without coarse laughter, without organs, separate from the Court and the Church on the one hand and the market square, alehouse, street and fairground on the other" (93-94). This place, "the town," was the public face of the private realm. "In the town, institutions of sociability and publicity were developed to counter those of the court, and it was there that the public sphere in the political realm emerged to confront the state" (Goodman 6).

"Public opinion," one would imagine, is the enunciation of the public sphere. The English phrase "dates back to the eighteenth century and has derived from the French *l'opinion publique*, which was first used in 1588 by Montaigne. "Adam Smith refers to it in his *Theory of Moral Sentiments* [1759], but it was Jeremy Bentham who developed the concept and concluded that "public opinion had the power to ensure that rulers would rule for the greatest happiness of the greater number" ("Public Opinion"). Louis XVI's finance minister, Jacques Necker, called it "an invisible power which, without treasures, without a bodyguard, and without an army gives laws to the city, to the court, and even to the palaces of kings" (Keane 166). The German sociologist Ferdinand Tönnies argued that public opinion has the equivalent social function in societies that religion has in communities ("Public Opinion"). Although many were optimistic about the liberating effects of public opinion, other social philosophers like Mill felt it as constraint: "Where for [William] MacKinnon public opinion is the engine for a liberal society, for Mill it brings social progress to a halt; public opinion stifles the 'vital' intellectual 'power' that would mark a truly liberalized public sphere . . . . Both writers identify public opinion as a technology of information: not as a particular set of opinions associated with one party or institution, nor as an actual representation of the body politic" (Stoddart 172).

"Theorists of the public and private," Anna Snaith writes, "invariably identify a historical period in which they feel the public sphere operated in its ideal state. Whether it be the Greek *polis* or the eighteenth-century, bourgeois public sphere, the idea is a place which operates under democratic law, to which all can gain access, in which all can speak freely and where society and government are critiqued and discussed" (6). Habermas's narrative is one of a rise and fall (an immediate fall, it would seem, perhaps coincident with its rise): the story of a public sphere gained by the liberal bourgeoisie of the nineteenth-century, for whom "the distinction between a public and a private realm is not just any old distinction but a constitutive one, for this separation expresses the notion--fundamental to liberalism--of the protection of individual freedom and the autonomy of persons" in the face of state interference; and lost "in the epoch of consumerism, mass media, and the expansion of the state into the intimate space of the family" (Rössler 2005:10 and Robbins viii). Whenever it fell, the public sphere exists no longer: it has been "refeudalized": transformed from a place of participatory debate into a strategy for manipulation. In this process, "the skills that empowered the public (rational-critical debate, participatory deliberation, etc.) are . . . relegated to the members of a small elite in an attempt to gain and centralize power" (Andrejevic 2004:39 and 40). This was a structural transformation "wrought by the fusion of corporate capitalism, the bureaucratic state, and a newly 'mediatized' public realm. This fusion creates the conditions for a pervasive manipulation and management of public opinion, which loses its critical function and becomes just one more input in 'the administered society'" (Villa 46). John Brewer puts it another way: around 1830, the place of rational-critical debate, the sphere where "property-owning private people" could meet as human beings, became infected by market forces because "the press became primarily a profit-seeking enterprise" (5). Still, commentators, witnessing the events of the recent "Arab Spring," would credit the new social media with laying the foundation for a new, satisfactory, public sphere.

Habermas's model has been energetically contested as everything from an historical stop-gap to an ideological ploy itself "that functioned to legitimate an emergent form of class rule" (Fraser 1993:8). Pauline Johnson objects that there never was such a place as Habermas's public sphere: "Its professed openness was illusory, scored by deep class divisions and powerful public interests" (27). Nancy Fraser similarly argues that the bourgeois public sphere was marked by a number of significant exclusions, namely, women and the poor: "this network of clubs and associations--philanthropic, civic, professional, and cultural--was anything but accessible to everyone. On the contrary, it was the arena, the training ground and eventually the power base of a stratum of bourgeois men who were coming to see themselves as a 'universal class' and preparing to assert their fitness to govern" (1993:6).

Putting it another way (after Oskar Negt and Alexander Kruge), there were many contending public spheres, "virtually contemporaneous with the bourgeois public there arose a host of competing counterpublics, including nationalist publics, popular peasant publics, elite women's publics, black publics, and working class publics" (Fraser 1997:61). But had anyone really believed in a single "phantasmal" public?[11] Even Habermas had admitted that it might only be a necessary fiction (Bartolovich 13). Jacques Derrida called public opinion "the silhouette of a phantom" (Robbins x).

According to the excellent taxonomy sketched by Jeff Weintraub, Habermas's public/private is in binary opposition to Alain Chartier's sociable/private and, according to Dena Goodman, both maps were produced in the same year, 1989, which saw the publication of English translations of the two works most closely associated with public sphere theory and the history of private life: Habermas's *The Structural Transformation of the Public Sphere*, and volume 3 of *A History of Private Life*, edited by Chartier (1).[12]

Sociability has an inverse relationship to family: "It is not individualism which has triumphed, but the family. But this family has advanced in proportion as sociability has retreated. It is as if the modern family had sought to take the place of the old social relationships (as these gradually defaulted) in order to preserve mankind from an unbearable moral solitude . . . . My central theme will be that when the city (and, earlier, the rural community) deteriorated and lost its vitality, the role of the family expanded like a hypertrophied cell" (Ariès in Weintraub 21 and 25).

The moral solitude that the family delivers us from in the city is the life beyond the window, the life on the streets; "uproar" is Dickens' term for it. As "the work of Henry Mayhew showed those who had been too blind to see, the streets outside the home were swarming with the poor, the plaintive, the caged, the cold, the hungry" (Chase 146).

A final map for human space (attached to the names of Arendt and Jacques Donzelot) has a third realm, the "social" ("the set of phenomena which sociology deals with"), "arising at the turn of the nineteenth century and abolishing the erstwhile public and private spheres": "It is a blurred ground between the old public and private, voiced as a field for intervention, love, and reform by socialists, conservatives, radicals, liberals, and feminists in their different and conjoined ways"-- "the reiterated sum of progressive philanthropies, theories of class, of poverty, of degeneration, studies of the domestic lives of workers"; "the body of peoples and political communities in the image of a family whose everyday affairs have to be taken care of by a gigantic, nation-wide administration of housekeeping" ("Anarchist," Riley 1988:49, and Snaith 7). "Once you depend upon charity all privacy is gone. The sanctity of the home is destroyed . . . . The investigator comes into the house unannounced any time of the day or night, questions anybody she finds in the house, criticizes the meals, the curtains" (Konrad Bercovici in Bergman 143). "Linda Gordon notes how child protective workers in the late nineteenth century visited homes of the poor late at night or early in the morning. If they were unable to gain entry, they actually climbed in windows" (Bergman 140). "Who today," Robert Musil wrote, "can still say that his anger is really his own anger, with so many people butting in and knowing much more about it than he does" (Rose 224).

> For Arendt, the most fundamental change [in modernity] is what she calls "the rise of the social" [or "civic housekeeping"] This development is primarily responsible for the fact that in modernity the private and public are no longer distinct, that politics has become merely a function of society and that the household has exploded the limits which formerly constrained it. As a result, the two realms now constantly flow into each other (Greve 15).

3. INVASIONS OF PRIVACY: SURVEILLANCE AND VOYEURISM

All men by nature desire to know.
Aristotle.

I begin this chapter on scrutiny with a reading of Herman Melville's *Moby Dick*. The romance has many fracture lines but above all it plays with a disjuncture between a narrative--Ahab's hunt for the white whale–and an anatomy–a heap of other chapters touching on whales and whaling. One way of dealing with this organizational mess is to ignore it, and many critics write about the book as if it were only Ahab's hunt. The obvious holding formula--that this is explanatory material, what you need to know about whales and the whaling industry in order to read the book--is inadequate. We don't need it. Every extended work of fiction engages some discursive environment (the law courts, the prisons, etc.) but almost none of them behave as this romance does. And there is simply too much of it; it competes with the narrative as if claiming equal authority as a bearer of significance. This discursive mass seems to consist of everything that has ever been represented about whales and whaling (even everything that has been written or drawn about things that *might be* whales). Certain extraneous chapters, like "The Whiteness of the Whale," "A Squeeze of the Hand" or "Fast Fish and Loose Fish" further suggest that the scope of the extra-fictional material should be doubled to include whaling as a privileged metaphor for everything else.

Wouldn't it be neat if the stuff that is not fiction also represented a quest? Surely something as threatening as the awful white whale cannot be hunted in only one puny way, as a time-bound pursuit with shafts of steel. If Ahab's hunt represents the Western will-to-power, then Ishmael's quest represents an equivalent will-to-knowledge.[2] The second hunt takes the form of an anatomy or encyclopedia, a counterpart to Ahab's obsession--as Ishmael himself suggests: "What am I that I should essay to hook the nose of this leviathan"--a need to know all about the whale, and, by knowing, to define and fix its meaning: "how shall we define the whale . . . so as conspicuously to label him for all time to come. To be short, then, a whale is *a spouting fish with a horizontal tail*. There you have him." Ishmael's intentions are infinite: "Since I have undertaken to manhandle this Leviathan, it behoves me to approve myself omnisciently exhaustive in the enterprise; not overlooking the minutest seminal germs of his blood, and spinning him out to the uttermost coil of his bowels." His desire to codify the whale is a particularly difficult task, as he himself admits: "It is some systematized exhibition of the whale in his broad genera, that I would now fain put before you. Yet is it no easy task. The classification of the constituents of a chaos, nothing less is here essayed." Ishmael begins his hunt in books, or, at least, someone who identifies himself as a sub-sub librarian tells us that he has "gone through the long Vaticans and street-stalls of the earth, picking up whatever random allusions to whales he could anyways find in any book whatsoever, sacred or profane" (1983:935, 936, 933, 1279 and 782). Not only bookstalls but every art gallery, every archaeological dig; every textual site in civilization.

Ishmael's expenditure of searching and cataloguing energy should remind us of the totalizing madness of Western philosophy, just as Ishmael's dissection of the whale resembles its investment in analysis. Melville makes it seem funny, but there is, as every good Romantic knew, a sharp weapon that penetrates more finely than the sharpest harpoon and kills more finally, and that is the analytical intelligence. A Romantic critique of knowledge as murder stretches from Samuel Taylor Coleridge to Henri Bergson, taking in Poe's "peering eyes" of science and Wordsworth's charge that "We murder to dissect" (Poe 1984b:38 and Wordsworth 56). Emily Dickinson "clearly echoes the Wordsworthian admonition," Fred White observes, when she writes in P 108,

> Surgeons must be very careful
> When they take the knife!
> Underneath their fine incisions
> Stirs the Culprit--*Life*!" (121).

Moby Dick deserves pride of place in this tradition of resistance to modern disenchantment.[1]

At the center of Melville's romance there is a dissection of the whale: a series of chapters ("The Battering Ram," "The Nut," "The Tail," "The Cassock," etc.) in which the whale is laid and sliced apart: "I confess," Ishmael tells us, "that since Jonah, few whalemen have penetrated very far beneath the skin of the adult whale; nevertheless I have been blessed with an opportunity to dissect him in miniature . . . . Think you I let that chance go, without using my boat-hatchet and jack-knife, and breaking the seal and reading all the contents of that young cub?" (1983:1271). Each part is held up and scrutinized, but Ishmael is finally forced to admit defeat: "Dissect him how I may, then, I but go skin deep; I know him not, and never will. But if I know not even the tail of this whale, how understand his head? much more, how comprehend his face, when face he has none? Thou shalt see my back parts, my tail, he seems to say, but my face shall not be seen" (1983:1271 and 1198).

In 1821, Washington Irving had written a tale in which an object of scrutiny rebukes an intrusive observer by turning his backside to him. The narrator of "The Stout Gentleman" is not an observer since the other he is obsessed with is out of sight, but he practices a second major mode of surveillance, acoustic. The narrator has taken sick on his travels and is convalescing one "rainy Sunday, in the gloomy month of November." He is on the verge of depression and desperately needs distraction. He hears the voice of a waiter saying that the stout gentleman in No. 13 wants his breakfast: "Here was a subject of speculation presented to my mind, and ample exercise for my imagination." Working from signs that are mostly audible (noises from overhead, conversation among the servants, etc.) the convalescent narrator tries to reconstruct the person of this individual. As the gentleman prepares to leave, the narrator springs out of bed and scrambles to the window: "This was the only chance I should ever have of knowing him . . . . [I] snatched aside the curtains, and just caught a glimpse of the rear of a person getting in at the coach-door . . . . and that was all I ever saw of the stout gentleman"; "The skirts of a brown coat parted behind, and gave me a full view of the broad disk of a pair of drab breeches" (49, 51 and 56).

There is no chapter on the whale's heart: "dissection is possible only on a dead body. Here lies the paradox and disappointment of anatomical dissection: the most powerful and privileged means of accessing the body cannot give access to its ultimate secret--life. The moment it gives access literally to its heart, the body forever closes the mystery of its life" (Lyu 314). The birth-mark in Hawthorne's tale seems to be a skin blemish, but when the scientist Aylmer dreams of removing it it shrinks inward until it coincides with his beloved's heart.

After the whale is dissected. Ishmael holds the stripped skeleton in his hands, as it were. His analysis can go no further, so he tosses the useless object over the side, where it floats to a bower in the Arsacides (the skeleton of the whale floats back to Typee). The natives discover it beached on the shore and immediately know, feelingly, that it is instinct with divinity and treat it as if it were a temple. Seeing this, Ishmael rushes there, pushing and thrusting his way through the worshipers, and does the only thing he can figure out to do: he measures the bones and their angles: "From their arrow-slit in the skull, the priests perceived me taking the altitude of the final rib. 'How now!' they shouted; 'Dar'st thou measure this our god!'" (1983:1273).

"How few things can a man measure with the tape of his understanding," H. D. Thoreau asks, but in a situation similar to Ishmael's the only thing that Hawthorne in "The Custom-House" can think to do to allay the power of the scarlet letter is to measure it (Thoreau 1990:192 and Tanner 47).

> "Yes, one day, after I had owned it [a guitar] a long time, a strange whim came into me. Thou know'st that it is not at all uncommon for children to break their dearest playthings in order to gratify a half-crazy curiosity to find out what is in the hidden heart of them . . . . Seized with this sudden whim, I unscrewed the part I showed thee, and peeped in, and saw 'Isabel'" (Melville 1984:177).

Aristotle announced at the beginning of his *Metaphysics* that all men desire to know, but the dangers associated with this desire, with curiosity, became first a dominant and then a minor strain in the Western intellectual tradition. Freud later reversed Aristotle's thesis: "All men by nature *do not* desire to know"--denaturalizing curiosity and making it a consequence of castration anxiety (Cho 194). Erasmus makes curiosity a sign of the fall:

> In the first golden age of the world there was no need of these perplexities; there was then no other sort of learning but what was naturally collected from every man's common sense . . . . and as to all the mysteries of providence, they made them rather the object of their wonder, than their curiosity; and therefore were not so presumptuous as to dive into the depths of nature, to labour for the solving all phenomena in astronomy, or to wrack their brains in the splitting of entities, and unfolding the nicest speculations, judging it a crime for any man to aim at what is put beyond the reach of his shallow apprehension.

"Curiosity is the most superficial of all the affections," Edmund Burke wrote in his treatise on the sublime, "it changes its object perpetually; it has an appetite which is very sharp, but very easily satisfied; and it has always an appearance of giddiness, restlessness, and anxiety." As opposed to wonder, its conventional opposite, it "has traditionally been identified with an appetite for knowledge and assimilated to the appetites of hunger and thirst" (Schmitt 127). In Voltaire's *Micromegas*, the astronaut from Sirius learns from the secretary of the Saturn Academy that the people on this planet have seventy-two senses and still complain daily that they possess so few: "We imagine more needs than we have, and with our seventy-two senses, our Saturn ring, and our five moons, we feel far too confined, since in spite of our curiosity and the numerous passions that result from our seventy-two senses, we still have plenty of time to get bored." The traveler from Sirius replies that in his homeland, where one has almost a thousand senses, it is no different, and there, also, subjects experience an undefined yearning and unrest (Blumenberg 405).

In Classical and Christian antiquity a series of legendary figures represented curiosity: Prometheus, Pandora, Icarus, Odysseus, Alexander, Psyche and Eve. In Mary Shelley's romance, Victor Frankenstein sees Eve, Psyche and Pandora as figures of overweening curiosity, and *Frankenstein* has often been read as a novel that condemns curiosity as the motive of those who transgress natural boundaries: "The world was to me a secret which I desired to divine. Curiosity, earnest research to learn the hidden laws of nature, gladness akin to rapture, as they were unfolded to me, are among the earliest sensations I can remember."

Eighteenth- and nineteenth-century European travelers had noted the invasive curiosity of Americans, and the narrators (or primary characters) in Poe, Hawthorne and Melville are very often driven by it. For Poe's narrators this trait is often a synonym for a perverseness which drives them to self-destruction, as in "Descent into the Maelstrom" where the narrator finds himself moved by a desire to observe and measure [an "unnatural curiosity"], as his "schooner-rigged smack" hovers on the verge of a deep oceanic vortex: "It may appear strange, but . . . I became possessed with the keenest curiosity about the whirl itself. I positively felt a *wish* to explore its depths, even at the sacrifice I was going to make" (1984b:443). And the narrator of "MS Found in a Bottle" tells us that "To conceive the horror of my sensations is, I presume, utterly impossible; yet a curiosity to penetrate the mysteries of these awful regions, predominates even over my despair, and will reconcile me to the most hideous aspect of death" (1984b:198).

The moral opposition in Hawthorne's fiction is between prying fed by curiosity and the respect morally due to others. The narrator of *The Blithedale Romance* reflects that "With the power, perhaps, to act in the place of destiny, and avert misfortune from my friends, I had resigned them to their fate. That cold tendency . . . which made me pry with a speculative interest into people's passions and impulses, appeared to have gone far towards unhumanizing my heart" (1983:767). The unpardonable sin for a character like Ethan Brand is to lose his sense of reverence for the human community and to observe the men and women around him with detached curiosity.

This crux is repeated in "Roger Malvin's Burial": Malvin has been badly wounded in a skirmish with Indians, and he tells his companion Reuben Bourne to leave him and get help. Reuben "began his solitary pilgrimage . . . . but after he had trodden far upon the rustling forest-leaves he crept back, impelled by a wild and painful curiosity, and, sheltered by the earthy roots of an uptorn tree, gazed earnestly at the desolate man" (1982:95). And the theme is echoed in an exchange between Holgrave the photographer and Phoebe Pyncheon in *House of the Seven Gables*. Holgrave presses the girl to describe to him Clifford Pyncheon's condition and she replies, "When he is cheerful–when the sun shines into his mind–then I venture to peep in, just as far as the light reaches, but no further. It is holy ground where the shadow falls!" "Had I your opportunities," Holgrave replies, "no scruples would prevent me from fathoming Clifford to the full depth of my plummet-line" (1983:505).

The epistemic pathway this chapter follows is that of seeing; about hearing too little will be said. The will to know through sight has long been a major trope in the conceptualization of scientific intelligence, and Romantic writing is full of phrases like "tearing the veil from nature" and "penetrating Nature's secrets." Two sites, nature and the human body, frustrated the gaze of scientists and physicians wanting to know their hidden contents and operations. The breakthrough mechanism in early modern medicine, according to Michel Foucault in *Birth of the Clinic*, was the "clinical gaze," "the probing, dissecting, and analytic" gaze that doctors learned to depend upon to diagnose and prescribe: "a gaze that burns things to their furthest truth . . . . as combustions reveal their secret only in the very vividness of fire" (Shapiro 161 and Foucault 1994:120). As Doctor John tells Lucy Snow in Charlotte Bronte's *Villette*, "I look on you now from a professional point of view, and I read, perhaps, all you would conceal--in your eye, which is curiously vivid and restless; in your cheek, which the blood has forsaken; in your hand, which you cannot steady" (355). .

Psychological sciences and moral studies also dreamed of looking inside the "head" and the "heart." Momus, the Greek god of censure, mocked Hephaestus for having made mankind without a door in its breast, through which thoughts could be seen, and Tristram Shandy wanted to fix Momus's glass in the human breast because then "nothing more would have been wanting, in order to have taken a man's character, but to have taken a chair and gone softly, as you would to a dioptrical bee-hive, and look'd in": "But this is not the case of the inhabitants of this earth;--our minds shine not through the body, but are wrapt up here in a dark covering of uncrystallized flesh and blood; so that if we would come to the specifick characters of them, we must go some other way to work" (Sterne 53 and Lucian).

Hawthorne's Roger Chillingworth is an exemplar of psychological gazing (although Hawthorne forces the ugliness of psychology to the surface by having Chillingworth be a cuckolded husband as well as an earnest healer). Early in his relationship with Arthur Dimmesdale, Chillingworth comes to understand that Dimmesdale's remarkable debility is not physical; he is repressing some powerful secret. Although the diagnostic moves that follow are presented as demonic activity, they anticipate the procedures of psychoanalysis: Chillingworth "strove to go deep into his patient's bosom, delving among his principles, prying into his recollections, and probing every thing with a cautious touch, like a treasure-seeker in a dark cavern" (1983:224).

The literary detective developed out of the Parisian *flaneur* who pretended, according to Walter Benjamin, "to read from faces [in the crowd] the profession, the ancestry, the character" of urban types (1999:429). Dana Brand suggests Addison and Steele's Spectator as an original *flaneur*, an observer "who is able to impose order, continuity, and coherence *in the act of watching* what appears to be chaotic," but, however far back one wants to take this, one of the central attributes of the type is extraordinary skill in the pseudo-science of physiognomy: reading a person's facial features and external characteristics for evidence of inner qualities (33). Poe's detective, C. Auguste Dupin, boasted, after Sterne, "with a low chuckling laugh, that most men, in respect to himself, wore windows in their bosoms" (1984b:401).[2]

Invasive seeing seemingly splits in two: surveillance and voyeurism. Surveillance is looking for secrets to enhance one's power, while voyeurism is looking for sexual pleasure. But of course this opposition is neither parallel nor sustainable; it is open to all sorts of logical booby traps. The sexual origin of epistemophilia which I previously ignored identifies surveillance with voyeurism. One may not be able to separate the two procedures at all, as witness Alfred Hitchcock's *Rear Window* and *Vertigo* (where a retired policeman gradually falls in love with the woman he's been hired to follow) or Poe's "Tell-Tale Heart" where the surveillance feels just like voyeurism. There and in Poe's "Man of the Crowd," surveillance has an erotic charge to it, as it so often does:

> With my brow to the glass, I was thus occupied in scrutinizing the mob, when suddenly there came into view a countenance . . . which at once arrested and absorbed my whole attention, on account of the absolute idiosyncrasy of its expression . . . . I felt singularly aroused, startled, fascinated. 'How wild a history,' I said to myself, 'is written within that bosom!' Then came a craving desire to keep the man in view--to know more of him. Hurriedly putting on an overcoat, and seizing my hat and cane, I made my way into the street, and pushed through the crowd in the direction which I had seen him take; for he had already disappeared (1984b:392-392).

In the following discussion on the nature and history of the surveillant and voyeuristic gaze, the latter will dominate simply because it has been so much more extensively theorized than the former.

The surveillant gaze is usually credited to Descartes; it is a cold visual exercise that leaves the subject intact and in possession of the object of the gaze, and this is reflected in most discursive formations as a power of the "seeing-man, a man who symbolizes the Euro-American male subject ": "he whose imperial eyes passively look out and possess" what they gaze at (Pratt 7). In many ways, modernity legitimized an essentially hostile look: before the appearance of omnibuses, railroads and streetcars in the nineteenth century, Georg Simmel notes, "men were not in a situation where for periods of minutes or hours they could or must look at each other without talking to one another" (360). James' Princess Casamassima always takes money with her when she goes "into the darkest places, the most fetid holes in London . . . . and always left it behind. She said, very naturally, that one couldn't go and stare at people, for an impression, without paying them, and she gave alms right and left" (1989:433).

But this gaze easily shades into the voyeuristic, or as it is often termed, the "male gaze." An important essay by Laura Mulvey, "Visual Pleasure and Narrative Cinema" (1973) anchored a theory of looking pleasure in Freud's *Three Essays on the Theory of Sexuality* where he argued that "visual impressions remain the most frequent pathway along which libidinal excitation is aroused" (7.156). Long before Freud, however, Aristotle married visual power and pleasure, beginning his *Poetics* with a paradox: noting that we take pleasure in seeing representations of objects that would terrify us in actuality, for example, a serpent sculpted in bronze.

Revisionary theories of the male gaze were offered by Jean-Paul Sartre and Jacques Lacan, but the Cartesian version continued in full force.[3] Although the major visual trajectory in modernism, according to Martin Jay, was anti-ocularism, the Cartesian gaze continued to exert almost total mastery over all production of narrative and most discursive formations and visual technologies. As Jay acknowledges, "Vision was still the privileged sense [in the fifties and sixties] but what that privilege produced in the modern world was damned as almost entirely pernicious" (384). The Cartesian gaze was now represented as a sinister and abusive, but all too powerful force.

Foucault, in *Discipline and Punish,* and Mulvey in her essay dwelled obsessively on the earlier tradition of looking even while they condemned it. Mulvey (along with John Berger and Christian Metz) is credited with transforming the Sartrean *regard* and the Lacanian gaze that render the subject weak and vulnerable into the cold and powerful gaze of Foucault's medical clinician and prison guard (see Krips). Mulvey's version of the male gaze was offered as the principle of power difference in narrative film. The audience (male and female) is bound up in the dominant perspective which combines the gaze of the male hero, the camera's movements and the strategies of the invisible (male) director. This look seeks out the eroticized presence of women and is supported by a plot that either victimizes or criminalizes these women for their sexuality.

In a section of his book on psychoanalysis and cinema, "Passion for Perceiving," Metz had argued that voyeurism, with its drive to master, is by nature sadistic (59-60). For Nietzsche, the "all-knowing, all-invading eyes" of God in *Zarathustra,* Carl Schneider claims, is "an image of rape, in which man is denuded of all protective covering, and his most private space penetrated without leave" (130). In Poe's "Oval Portrait," the intense gaze of the artist, directed at the beloved woman he is painting, is depicted as vampiric as it literally transfers her to canvas, feature by feature, and in so doing drains the vitality of the living woman. In Hawthorne, this murderous gaze belongs to both the artist and the scientist. The painter in Hawthorne's "Prophetic Pictures" has the power to pry into the souls of his sitters and to depict in his painting their future misdeeds and tragedies: "It is an awful gift" (1982:456). The look is fatal in "The Birth-Mark" where Georgina "soon learned to shudder" beneath her scientist husband's clinical gaze: "It needed but a glance, with the peculiar expression that his face often wore, to change the roses of her cheek into a deathlike paleness, amid which the Crimson Hand was brought strongly out, like a bas-relief of ruby on the whitest marble" (1982:766-767).[4]

Since antiquity, this sadistic male gaze had circulated through discourse and representation as the evil eye or the basilisk stare: "The Gilgamesh Epic speaks of the demon *utukku,* who by a mere glance could cause injury to a man" and "Philostratus, in his biography of Apollonius of Tyana, recorded that the famed magus possessed such wonderful eyes that he could kill with a mere glance" (Tourney 479-480).

In the nineteenth century this power was restyled mesmerism, in, for example, Hawthorne's *House of the Seven Gables*--

> Now, the wizard's grandson, the young Matthew Maule of our story, was popularly supposed to have inherited some of his ancestor's questionable traits . . . . He was fabled, for example, to have a strange power of getting into people's dreams, and regulating matters there according to his own fancy, pretty much like the stage-manager of a theatre. There was a great deal of talk among the neighbors, particularly the petticoated ones, about what they called the witchcraft of Maule's eye. Some said that he could look into people's minds; others, that, by the marvelous power of this eye, he could draw people into his own mind, or send them, if he pleased, to do errands to his grandfather, in the spiritual world; others, again, that it was what is termed an Evil Eye, and possessed the valuable faculty of blighting corn, and drying children into mummies with the heart-burn–

and also in *Blithedale Romance* and Poe's "The Facts in the Case of M. Valdemar" and "Mesmeric Revelations" (1983:515). In these fictions, mesmerism figures as the ultimate invasion of privacy since it produces a profound sympathy between the hypnotist and his subject: the former invades the body and soul of the latter and produces any effects he wills, including, in "Valdemar," the physical positioning of the body (1984b:837). In *Gables*, Hawthorne brings mesmerism into the industrial age by identifying it with photography.

An opposition between the gaze and a sidelong glance runs through Romantic literature, between an invasive and destructive force and a gentler, more spiritual mode of being in the world. In "Murders in the Rue Morgue," the Chevalier Dupin offers the following analogy for proper detective work:

> To look at a star by glances--to view it in a side-long way, by turning toward it the exterior portions of the *retina* . . . is to behold the star distinctly--is to have the best appreciation of its luster--a luster which grows dim just in proportion as we turn our vision *fully* upon it. . . . it is possible to make even Venus herself vanish from the firmament by a scrutiny too sustained, too concentrated, or too direct (1984b:412).

Despite its supposed roots in optics, Poe's statement sounds suspiciously like an aesthetic, or even a moral, allegory. The sidelong glance is a glance that nourishes beauty as opposed to the gaze, which dims or destroys it; and beauty is the object of the poetry and the great theme of his horror tales: "the death, then, of a beautiful woman is, unquestionably, the most poetical topic in the world" (1984a:19).[5]

The aesthetics of the sidelong glance are also important to Hawthorne, particularly in *The Marble Faun*, where he writes that "It is a peculiarity of this picture [a portrait of Beatrice Cenci], that its profoundest expression eludes a straightforward glance, and can only be caught by side glimpses, or when the eye falls casually upon it" (1983:1040-1041). Later in the book the sculptor Kenyon proposes to sculpt the head of the "faun," Donatello, in marble. The sitter tells the sculptor that it "troubles me to be looked at steadfastly," and Kenyon tells him that that will be no hindrance to his work, "for I will catch the likeness and expression by side-glimpses, which (if portrait painters and bust-makers did but know it) always brings home richer results than a broad stare" (1983:1040-1041).

Most surveillance is conducted by the state, which is driven by an inordinate desire to know all. In earlier ages state surveillance may have been limited in its aim, as, for instance, a method for hunting criminals; but the need for indiscriminate surveillance grew up in the West in the nineteenth century along with the growth of urban centres which lacked the family and community networks that previously held individuals in place. Cities were places where anonymity "became a new condition of life" (Simmel in Veel 2).

It was not only the learned professional (physician or psychologist) who deployed the surveillant gaze, it was the lunatic and lover as well. Acute visual surveillance was also the mark of the paranoiac or other mental sufferer (like the lover) whose psychological condition generated feverish watchfulness. Paranoia is often figured as a continual assault on our privacy, while obsession and infatuation turn us all into secret agents;

> At every other period in his life, the little everyday words and actions of another person had always seemed wholly valueless to Swann . . . . But in this strange phase of love the personality of another person becomes so enlarged, so deepened, that the curiosity which he could now feel aroused in himself, to know the least details of a woman's daily occupation, was the same thirst for knowledge with which he had once studied history. And all manner of actions, from which, until now, he would have recoiled in shame, such as spying, to-night, outside a window, to-morrow, for all he knew, putting adroitly provocative questions to casual witnesses, bribing servants, listening at doors, seemed to him, now, to be precisely on a level with the deciphering of manuscripts, the weighing of evidence, the interpretation of old monuments, that was to say, so many different methods of scientific investigation, each one having a definite intellectual value and being legitimately employable in the search for truth (Proust 210).

"The jealous are condemned to live in that thorny place where surveillance is born," Michel Serres writes, "a jalousie is a place from which one watches" (31). Modern systems of surveillance bear an uncanny resemblance to these moods and pathologies, suspicion and paranoia, that had long been proscribed by psychology. Suspicion seems to give me the right to violate the privacy of others, as in Hitchcock's *Rear Window*, while surveillance creates suspicion: "The power to observe, by itself, induces in the observer the sense that the observed is ambiguous or pathological. One is placed under constant suspicion just by being placed under constant watchfulness" (Kateb 274).

A new type of surveillance, a massive policing power "begins to permeate" Western societies from the end of the eighteenth century (D. A. Miller 17). In *Discipline and Punish*, Foucault identified this power with "an ideal of unseen but all-seeing surveillance, which, though partly realized in several . . . institutions, is identified with none" (Miller viii). Such a negative vision of the power of the state apparatus abolishes any realm of privacy. Foucault is the theorist of this modern surveillance which he understands as a disciplinary power produced through the dynamics of the visibility of the many to the few. And he found his pure model in a panoptic prison envisioned by Jeremy Bentham in 1785, which consisted of a tower surrounded by cells within which prisoners are clearly visible at all times. Because the prisoners are never certain when or if they are being watched (one of the first details Winston Smith shares about the telescreens in *1984* is that there was "no way of knowing whether you were being watched at any given moment . . . . You had to live--did live, from habit that became instinct--in the assumption that every sound you made was overheard, and, except in darkness, every movement scrutinized"), the disembodied guard becomes god-like in presence and authority, and all good things followed: "Morals reformed–health preserved–industry invigorated–instruction diffused–public burthens lightened," Bentham wrote, "Economy seated, as it were, upon a rock–the gordian knot of the Poor Laws are not cut, but untied–all by a simple idea in Architecture!" (Orwell 4-5 and Ainley 88). And, Foucault wrote, this "system of surveillance . . . involves very little expense. There is no need for arms, physical violence, material constraints. Just a gaze." Foucault regarded Bentham as a complement to Rousseau, since the latter dreamed of democracy as transparent: "It was the dream that each individual, whatever position he occupied, might be able to see the whole of society" (1980:155).

"At the beginning of the nineteenth century," he declared, "the great spectacle of physical punishment disappeared" and Western civilization moved from a society of spectacle to one of surveillance, a modern power that replaced "violence and force of arms with the more gentle constraint of uninterrupted visibility" (1977:14 and 217 and Fraser 1981:278).[6] The power deployed was virtually invisible: "It keeps a low profile. It has no need of the spectacular displays characteristic of the exercise of power in the *ancien regime*" (Fraser

1981:278). The result is that "We are neither in the amphitheater, nor on the stage, but in the panoptic machine, invested by its effects of power" (Foucault 1979:217). Panoptic civilization neatly reverses the previous scopic regime, the principle of which was "To render accessible to a multitude of men the inspection of a small number of objects." Conversely, the principle of the new era Is "To procure for a small number, or even for a single individual, the instantaneous view of a great multitude" (Foucault 1979:216).

The regime of spectacle was followed by a grand but silent shift toward interiority and secrecy and a redefinition of punishment as spiritual discipline. All institutions in what Foucault calls "the disciplinary society" are modeled on this panoptic scheme; all are "like a faceless gaze that transformed the whole social body into a field of perception: thousands of eyes posted everywhere, mobile attentions ever on the alert" (1979:214).

The guards in the panoptic prison represent all-seeing eyes, an image of total surveillance dating at least from Nicholas of Cusa in the fifteenth century--he sent to the monks at Tegernsee a portrait so cleverly painted that the viewer always had the impression that the figure was gazing back at him–including along the way the Freudian superego and the recruiting sergeant whose eyes follow you everywhere, Santa Claus who knows if you've been naughty or nice, and the teacher with eyes in the back of her head. Many religious societies imagine gods that are always watching: "'The eye of God *is* on you,' said the officer, sternly seating himself; 'and so is another eye, to which he has deputed the sleepless vigilance and resistless penetration of his own,–the eye of the holy office'" (Maturin).

The panoptic prison was Foucault's model for this system, but the modern world consisted of an extensive series of metaphoric panopticons--the schoolroom, the hospital, the prison, the airport where "everything must be seen and all must be shown"--fields of surveillance or sites of written reports constituting a database (Weibel 207). After Foucault, many cultural systems were reread as panoptic structures: maps, the early modern novel, "the social scientific projects of the enlightenment like Comte's social physics, the Protestant ethic as described by Weber, and Durkheim's social solidarity" (Margolis). Mark Koch identifies Western cartography after the Renaissance as a prime instance, as "atlases and maps now made it possible to hold in one's hands simulacra of the earth and to behold with the eye the kingdoms of the world."

According to Zygmunt Bauman, we are currently in the grip of a system that disciplines us to be consumers, seducing us into the market economy (33). David Collings would have Malthus, not Bentham, exemplify the shift to this postmodern regime, "for he advocates using the market to impose an intractable discipline on ordinary people . . . . Malthusian discipline makes Benthamite surveillance redundant" (20). According to Gilles Deleuze, after 1945 we moved beyond panopticism into a "society of control." In the previous "disciplinary societies" (eighteenth to twentieth centuries),

> the individual never ceases passing from one closed environment to another, each having its own laws: first the family; then the school . . . then the barracks . . . then the factory; from time to time the hospital; possibly, the prison . . . . And now, another transition is taking place. This transition is not complete, but it began shortly after WWII. In this new society, which we can call the society of control, the closed environments . . . are given way to different forms of power. These control societies control the population with new technologies, molecular engineering, genetic manipulation, and so forth (Deleuze 3 and Shawver).

Thomas Matthiessen proposes a complementary form of universal surveillance, synopticism, a regime brought about by the mass media and television where, again, the few are displayed to the many. The disciplinary effect that follows is not a result of surveillance but, rather, of the implanting of false consciousness (215).[7]

Surveillance and voyeurism supported another institution--eighteenth- and nineteenth-century fiction--as motif and, as D. A. Miller wrote in his critical study of this policing project, *The Novel and the Police*, as agency and structure. In a neat split, the British novel devoted itself, with some exceptions, to surveillance; the American romance, exceptions again, to voyeurism.

Miller argues that the novel was a crucial tool in the apparatus that produced the docile bodies that the century desired. His exemplary texts are Wilkie Collins' *Moonstone* and *Woman in White*, Dickens's *Bleak House* (with a nod to *Oliver Twist* and *David Copperfield*), and Trollope's *Barchester Towers*.[8] The police of his title is primarily the affective mechanism put in place to discipline the home and family ("a station house that now is everywhere, even or especially in the novel one reads at home"), so that there is no need for official police interference: "Whenever the novel censures policing power, it has already reinvented it, in *the very practice of novelistic representation* (Miller xii and 20).

The novel had come into being as a literary genre that enshrined privacy, and both Miller and Brooks before him are alive to the irony whereby the novel violates this privacy in the act of protecting it. By its very nature as a publication (but even more as a fiction), the novel breaches the privacy it presumes to speak for, while proclaiming all the while its devotion to the sanctity of privacy:

> The Gaiety of *Tom's* Temper suited better with *Sophia*, than the grave and sober Disposition of Master *Blifil*. And the Preference which she gave the former of these, would often appear so plainly, that a Lad of a more passionate Turn than Master *Blifil* was, might have shown some Displeasure at it. As he did not, however, outwardly express any such Disgust, it would be an ill Office in us to pay a Visit to the inmost Recesses of his Mind, as some scandalous People search into the most secret Affairs of their Friends, and often pry into their Closets and Cupboards, only to discover their Poverty and Meanness to the World (104).

Miller gives this irony several more turns of the screw:

> Perhaps the most fundamental value that the Novel, as a cultural institution, may be said to uphold is privacy, the determination of an integral, autonomous, "secret" self. Novel reading takes for granted the existence of a space in which the reading subject remains safe from the surveillance, suspicion, reading and rape of others. Yet this privacy is always specified as the freedom to read about characters who oversee, suspect, read, and rape one another. It is not just that, strictly private subjects, we read about violated,

> objectified subjects but that, in the very act of reading about them, we contribute largely to constitute them as such. We enjoy our privacy in the act of watching privacy being violated, in the act of watching that is already itself a violation of privacy (162).

Poe had already taken this relationship through a turn in his "Philosophy of Composition" [1848]. Because the novel, unlike the lyric poem, cannot be read at a single sitting, reading is invariably interrupted: "the affairs of the world interfere" (1984a:15). Novel reading thus participates in the opposition between private and public in two ways: it's a private place to which we retire to read about the world at large, but that world regularly interrupts the reading.

According to Brooks, this had all been worked out in the novels of Samuel Richardson. They provide the "most typical manifestation of this overdetermined privacy of the novel," and what is dramatized in them is the "violation of that privacy figured as a rape of a woman in her boudoir": "Although in retrospect we learn that Mr. B. has been intercepting and reading her letters from the first, Pamela's habit of hiding them in her bosom or sewing them into her underclothes encourages him to assault both forms of privacy at once" (Brooks 30 and Yeazell 124).

At the beginning of the English novel, we find a monster of surveillance in the person of Robinson Crusoe, a ruthlessly single-minded hero who scrutinizes every element in his environment for its place in his overriding schemes of survival and prosperity. The novel pretends that it is all about material acquisition, but it is also about something else, something for which there is little overt logic in the text. Once cast away upon his desert island, Crusoe is seized by crippling anxiety: he fears invasion, and he works frantically to protect himself by enclosing himself in ever tighter containers (walls, doors, caves, tents, shrubs, fences)--culminating in what Peter Hulme calls "a byzantine fortress of monumental solidity" (193). When this activity does not bring him the ease he desires, he ratchets his anxiety up to the next level: not self-enclosure but self-erasure. As if the theme of a man marooned on an uninhabited island were not a sufficiently dark symbol of privacy, compulsive hiding is added.[9]

Crusoe is tormented by the notion that he might be observed or sighted. In a second beginning of the English novel, William Godwin's *Caleb Williams*, the hero is just the opposite, obsessively curious, both in general--

> The spring of action which, perhaps more than any other, characterized the whole train of my life, was curiosity . . . . I could not rest till I had acquainted myself with the solutions that had been invented for the phenomena of the universe. In fine, this produced in me an invincible attachment to books of narrative and romance. I panted for the unraveling of an adventure with an anxiety, perhaps almost equal to that of the man whose future happiness or misery depended on its issue–

and in particular--"The more impenetrable Mr. Falkland was determined to be, the more uncontrollable was my curiosity . . . . a kind of fatal impulse, that seemed destined to hurry me to my destruction" (60, 181 and 198).

It makes generic sense that narrators should be formed around a desire to know, leading to compulsive surveillance. Such is the case of the prying narrators in the short fiction of Poe and Hawthorne: the narrator in "The Tell-Tale Heart" who devotes all the time and energy of the tale to imaginatively and actually peering at an old man who lies dying in an adjacent room, or Wakefield in the tale of that name (the narrative focus if not the narrator) who leaves his family, takes an apartment in an adjacent block and spends the next twenty years imagining how they were passing the time.[10]

Such was also the case, before the rise of the short story and the novel, in serial periodicals like the *Spectator*. Addison's Spectator has an "insatiable thirst after knowledge" and has "looked into the highest and lowest of mankind and made shrewd guesses at the inmost thoughts and reflections of all whom I behold." In Elizabeth Heywood's *Invisible Spy*, the narrator has been provided with a "belt of Invisibility" and an early form of tape recorder (Merritt 185).

Caleb Williams's adversary, Squire Falkland, moves surveillance to another register and intensity. He or his surrogates are figures of unrelenting pursuit and persecution, like Victor Hugo's Javert, figures of all-seeing vigilance and avenging fury: "Whithersoever I removed myself, it was not long before I had occasion to perceive this detested adversary [Falkland's agent or detective, Gines] in my rear . . . . never could I count upon an instant's security; never could I wrap myself for a moment in the shroud of oblivion" (411). Describing his composition of the novel, Godwin relates finding a "tremendous compilation, entitled 'God's Revenge against Murder,' where the beam of the eye of Omniscience was represented as perpetually pursuing the guilty and laying open his most hidden retreats to the light of day," and Williams's nemesis is envisioned as just such an avenger : "Did his power reach through all space, and his eye penetrate every concealment?" (449 and 335-336). Javert, too, was like "an eye always fixed on Monsieur Madeleine. An eye full of suspicion and conjecture": "His stare was cold and piercing as a gimlet. His whole life was contained in these two words: waking and watching. He marked out a straight path through the most tortuous thing in the world . . . . and he was a spy as others are priests" (175).

Mme. Beck in *Villette*, Count Fosco in *Woman in White* and John Claggart in *Billy Budd* are actual or metaphoric spymasters. Bronte's novel and Melville's novella are both mantled in the affective mythology of the French Reign of Terror and Napoleon's subsequent creation of the spy system. Mme. Beck represents both the efficient spy system of the Napoleonic regime and the inquisitorial practices of Catholicism. Lucy Snow, the narrator of the novel, compares her to a superintendent of police: "She glides around spying at keyholes, oiling the doors, imprinting keys, opening drawers, carefully scrutinizing Lucy's memorabilia and turning . . . [Lucy's] pockets inside out" ("'Surveillance', 'espionage,' -- these were her watch-words") (Gilbert 408 and Bronte 99). Claggart, "a peculiar ferreting genius," is in charge of security on board the *Bellipotent* at a particularly unstable moment during Britain's war against Napoleonic France (1984:1375). Count Fosco, on the other hand, is associated with Italian secret societies during the Risorgimento as well as Freemasonry; he styles himself the "Perpetual Arch-Master of the Rosicrucian Masons of Mesopotamia" (591).

The novels at the core of Miller's study were also instrumental in the formation of detective fiction, and spying, tracking and hunting are of course central to that turn of the century project which takes mystery or crime to be an invitation for excesses of surveillance:

> In detective fiction the relation between seeing and policing is taken for granted; literally, the range of the detective's vision is the range of his power. That power operates by placing the entire world of the text under scrutiny and under surveillance and invokes the possibility of an absolute supervision, in which everything may be comprehended and "policed" (Seltzer 50-51).

In detective fiction, crimes also oblige the investigator to invade the most private recesses of the victim's life (rummage through his or her family secrets and the secrets of his or her class) (Fillingham 670).[11]

The other side of such obsessive watchfulness is paranoia, the feeling of being watched by unseen eyes. An early moment in British fiction, the Gothic, was given over to this condition, and *Caleb Williams* features extremities of both surveillance and paranoia. An associated fictional genre, the thriller, is also steeped in a paranoia that is justified by the ubiquity and consummate perfection in surveillance of the conspiratorial organization that generates the mystery and the excitement. In Robert Louis Stevenson's *The Dynamiter*, for example, the woman who believes that she has escaped from the Mormons finds them behind every facade on her journey back to London: "In every place, on every side, the most unlikely persons, man or woman, rich or poor, became . . . spies to observe and regulate my conduct." Of the equally adept Mormons of *A Study in Scarlet*, Doyle writes, "The victims of persecution had now turned persecutors . . . of the most terrible description. Not the Inquisition of Seville, nor the German Verhmgericht, nor the secret societies of Italy, were ever able to put a more formidable machinery in motion . . . . Its invisibility . . . made this organization doubly terrible. It appeared to be omniscient and omnipotent, and yet was neither seen nor heard" (62).

Proust epitomized the voyeuristic regard as follows: "I gazed at her . . . with that gaze which is not merely a messenger from the eyes, but in whose window all the senses assemble and lean out, petrified and anxious, that gaze which would fain reach, touch, capture, bear off in triumph the body at which it is aimed, and the soul with the body" (108). In the Western tradition, voyeurism had long been regarded as sinful, often punishable by blindness or bestial transformation. Tiresias, for example, is blinded for looking at two snakes coupling, for looking at Artemis in her bath, and for seeing the naked bosom and limbs of Athene. In the *Golden Ass* Lucian is turned into an ass for spying on Venus bathing in the sea. "The beautiful legend of Lady Godiva," Freud writes, "tells how all the town's inhabitants hid behind their shuttered windows, so as to make easier the lady's task of riding naked through the streets in broad daylight, and how the only man who peeped through the shutters at her revealed loveliness was punished by going blind" (11.217). In other voyeur myths, such as Actaeon and Diana or Susannah and the Elders, Daniel Donoghue writes, the punishment is death (105).

No American author was as deeply invested in voyeurism as Nathaniel Hawthorne. From the time of an early sketch, "Sights from a Steeple," he was obsessed with the equation of narration and visual intrusion. In this sketch, the narrator is identified with the eponymous Paul Pry as he looks over the roofs of the dwellings from his perch high on a church steeple, knowing that within each of those shells there is a story worth telling, and he yearns to appropriate all these secrets and shames:

> O that the multitude of chimneys could speak, like those of Madrid, and betray, in smoky whispers, the secrets of all who, since their first foundation, have assembled at the hearths within! O that the Limping Devil of Le Sage would perch beside me here, extend his wand over this contiguity of roofs, uncover every chamber, and make me familiar with their inhabitants! The most desirable mode of existence might be that of a spiritualized Paul Pry (1982:43).[12]

The first thing that Herman Melville tells us in his first romance, *Typee*, is that a book is a look: he subtitles the fiction of his stay in an island paradise a "Peep at Polynesian Life." The book is not merely a look but an unseemly look, and the pun on peeping Tom (Tom or Tommo being the narrator's name) operates throughout.[13]

What holds for *Typee* should be thinkable for travel literature and anthropology in general. A Melville critic, Robert K. Martin, acknowledges that in Melville's era of Western colonialism, the popular travel narrative functioned as "genteel pornography" ("the role of the travel narrative was taken on in the twentieth century by *National Geographic* magazine") (18). I would characterize traditional anthropology as the "science" that allowed male authorities and their students to look at naked women without needing to register embarrassment or shame.

At the "beginning" of Anthropology, James Frazer, and Freud after him, looked at primitive society and saw incest at the center of everything. Frazer looked out into the contemporary countryside and saw folks fucking--"At the present day it might perhaps be vain to look in civilized Europe for customs of this sort . . . . But ruder races in other parts of the world have consciously employed the intercourse of the sexes as a means to ensure the fruitfulness of the earth; and some rites which are still, or were till lately, kept up in Europe can be reasonably explained only as stunted relics of a similar practice" (136).

Even more than American romance, narrative film has been identified as the territory of the voyeuristic male gaze as outlined by Metz, Mulvey and Berger. Charlie Chaplin's *City Lights* contains two adjacent scenes of a high sexual density that are never anchored in the script, two scenes featuring sculptural nudes, one monumental and one minuscule. If Charlie is infantile in the first of these scenes (he lies asleep in the arms of a large maternal statue as it is being unveiled), he is a voyeur in the second, standing in front of a plate-glass window which displays a nude female torso as well as other "antiques." Charlie pretends to be absorbed by an equestrian statue next to it. Still, he glances at the torso from time to time but dissembles his interest by making gestures of art evaluation that signify he is only doing art-looking not sex-looking.

Classic American film usually allows us (male and female) to look at the body of a woman who signifies desire and to act as if we owned her: the film collaborates in our wishes and delivers her up to us through both spectacle and story. The great cinema artist of the voyeuristic impulse was Alfred Hitchcock (after he came to America), and the primary examples of this art act are *Rear Window* and *Vertigo*. The first film is actually a curious blend of voyeurism and surveillance, opening on a domestic panopticon, a central apartment that looks out on a courtyard flanked by an array of other apartment windows. The protagonist, L. B. Jeffries [Jimmy Stewart], is an immobilized photographer who eases his boredom by innocently spying on his neighbors: "He is the warden . . . in a private panopticon which involves, as Foucault said: 'so many cages, so many small theaters, in which each actor is alone, perfectly individualized and constantly visible'" (Stam 197). Jeff's fireplace mantle displays the fruits of his earlier voyeurism: glamour pinups and disaster photos.[14]

The most explicit statement of the relationship between voyeurism and sadism (the male gaze) comes in the British film *Peeping Tom* (1960), which identifies both voyeurism and surveillance with homicidal violence. The film tells the story of the short life of Mark Lewis, an obsessive photographer who works in film and TV. In his spare time he murders women while photographing them, acting out a childhood trauma induced by his psychiatrist father. Mark forces the victims to watch themselves dying in a mirror that is attached to his camera. *Peeping Tom*'s American counterpart was *Psycho*, produced in the same year by an artist, Alfred Hitchcock, who resembled Michael Powell in many ways, and it is also devoted to the repositioning of voyeurism with eroticized violence rather than erotic pleasure.

4. THE EROSION OF PRIVACY

> The primitive conquerors were satisfied with outward submission; they did not inquire into the private lives or local customs of their victims . . . the conquerors of today are resolved to gaze over the level surface of their empire and to encounter no deviation from uniformity.
>
> Benjamin Constant

> There is no corner and no night. A relentless inquisition [the power of the newspaper] drags every secret to the day, turns the glare of this solar microscope on every malfaisance, so as to make the public a more terrible spy than any foreigner.
>
> Ralph Waldo Emerson

The Anderson Tapes, a 1971 film by Sidney Lumet, presents in detail the robbing of an upscale New York City apartment building on Labor Day weekend by a team of specialist criminals. Each of them, however, is under constant surveillance by one security agency or another: there is a private detective eavesdropping on Anderson's girlfriend because she is also the mistress of a wealthy man; the Bureau of Narcotics and Dangerous Drugs is keeping tabs on a team member who is a released drug dealer; the FBI investigating the Black activist; and the IRS watching the mob boss financing the operation. Because the various agencies are not in communication with one another none of them is even aware that a robbery is being planned. Total surveillance fails to see or hear the key dangled before their collective eyes and ears.

Irony aside, the film also demonstrates how easy and pervasive electronic intrusion is. Like the felons in the film, we have all, in fact or potentially, been under surveillance for some time, so much so that the "extent and techniques of surveillance, record-keeping, and publicity wielded by government, medical authorities, marketing agencies, and telecommunications media overwhelm inherited expectations of a divide between public and private" (Fox 542). John Turner sees a "hemorrhaging of privacy in late capitalist cultures" on various fronts: "Privacy is traded away for security in a society encouraged to be reactionary and paranoid by the sensational imagery of the evening news. Privacy is invaded for pleasure by the sleazy content of the talk show/confessional circuit, the desire to gaze and be gazed upon . . . . And privacy is exploited for profit in the freemarket swapping of massive personal databases" (107). So it is not surprising that opinion polls show that individual privacy is an overriding concern of the citizenry, but it's an idle concern. "You already have zero privacy--get over it," warned Scott McNealy, chief executive of Sun Microsystems, at the launch of his company's Jini consumer networking software in 1999 (Glancy 1). When did privacy end? Deborah Nelson finds it ending in the 1966 "Starr Report" and six months before that--"a grisly death"--in Diana's fatal car crash: "Privacy, it seems, is not simply dead. It is dying over and over again" since the 1950s (xi).

We leak information as we move through our day, or, to change metaphors: "We each leave 'digital footprints' that can be tracked by data mining companies and used to create purchasing profiles, medical summaries, political agendas, and the like" (Adam Moore 365):

> People give away vast amounts of valuable information about themselves, wittingly or unwittingly, by using credit cards, signing up for supermarket discount programs, joining frequent-flyer clubs, sending e-mail, browsing on the Internet, using electronic tollbooth passes, mailing in rebate forms, entering sweepstakes, and calling toll-free numbers. Such behaviors are essentially voluntary (although a somewhat abstract case can be made that they are the product of what has been called "the tyranny of

> convenience"), but many other ways of participating in everyday life basically *require* the divulging of information about oneself (Lester 28).[1]

The landmark article on the right to privacy published in 1890 by Warren and Brandeis had been a response to recent technological developments such as hand-held photography. The Olmstead of *Olmstead v. U. S.* (1928) was a Seattle bootlegger whose conviction resulted from federal wiretapping. For a majority of the Court, telephone wires, "reaching to the whole world from the defendant's house or office . . . . are not part of his house or office, any more than are the highways along which they are stretched." Brandeis, however, argued that the "Fourth Amendment must adapt to a changing world":

> ". . . time works changes, brings into existence new conditions and purposes." Subtler and more far-reaching means of invading privacy have become available to the Government . . . . [and] the progress of science in furnishing the Government with means of espionage is not likely to stop with wiretapping. Ways may some day be developed by which the Government, without removing papers from secret drawers, can reproduce them in court, and by which it will be enabled to expose to a jury the most intimate occurrences of the home (*Olmstead*).

As it develops and expands, technology opens up greater areas and opportunities for the invasion of privacy. The coming of the computer eroded much of the privacy protection in place: caller ID, mandatory and random drug testing, thermal imaging devices, "Surveillance photos like those commonly taken of those using Fast Lane, resulting in tickets mailed to speeding offenders and similar photos are now taken at red lights . . . . Face scanning . . . at casinos, and at large sporting events . . . matches those photos with database records of felons, etc. (De Cew).

And technology outstrips and overwhelms legal attempts to stem its potential for privacy violation.[2] But privacy is also a product of technology, of modern conveniences like the telephone, television, washer, dryer, air conditioner, etc., which conduce to greater self-sufficiency in the home. Anti-privacy technology and privacy technology chase one another in accelerating spirals, so much so that today privacy is a billion-dollar commodity and "as privacy becomes rarer and rarer," Watts Wacker and Jim Taylor prophecy, "it will assume greater and greater worth, and privacy management will become one of the great growth industries of the twenty-first century" (122).

Surveillance is an invariable project of the sovereign state, whether secular or religious. As Aristotle also wrote, "A tyrant should endeavor to know what each of his subjects says or does, and should employ spies" (2.2085). Foundation fictions of the state declare that the individual originally possessed full rights and traded them away to the collective for security. In the liberal state, the individual's right of privacy had always been in some balance with the state's right to know until after 9/11 when the see-saw ended in an almost complete victory for the latter.

In the twentieth century, state surveillance expanded into what has come to be called the surveillance state. Early models for such regimes were theocracies, like the Puritan community in early New England. Moral scrutiny was not only the prerogative of the community, which it exercised forcefully, but also the obligation of each individual, as Robert Browne wrote in 1582: "We must all watch one another and try out wickedness" (Robert Smith 8). The preeminent surveillance states of the twentieth century were the totalitarian states of Germany and the Soviet Union, but the liberal democracies soon helplessly imitated them. While proclaiming its democratic tolerance, America adopted these measures as cold-war strategies to combat or contain Soviet Communism (which had adopted many of its own security measures as a result of the pressure of Western espionage and militarism); as Deborah Nelson writes, "the cold war had created a rationale for surveillance that was infinitely expandable" (11). The modern state has been fanatical about its possible insecurity and information is collected and protected beyond any logic.

Through the late twentieth century, America had seen itself as a place where individual freedom and domestic privacy flourished. The opposite condition was the conventional index of the two great modern totalitarian states. In *Origins of Totalitarianism*, Arendt argued that "extinguishing private space was totalitarianism's fundamental innovation in the form of domination," and the democracies prided themselves that the sanctity of the private realm was what most distinguished them from totalitarian governments (Nelson 9 and xiii). V. I. Lenin told the Young Communists in 1920, "we recognize nothing private. Our morality is entirely subordinate to the interests of the class struggle," while in

1930, Robert Ley said of the Nazi regime, "The only person who is still a private citizen in Germany is somebody who is asleep" (Bryant 76 and Lyon 185-186).

Orwell's Emmanuel Goldstein declared in *1984*: "By comparison with that existing today, all the tyrannies of the past were half-hearted and inefficient" because "in the past no government had the power to keep its citizens under constant surveillance" (214). There is almost constant surveillance in this novel's thinly disguised version of the Stalinist state: "Any sound that Winston [Smith] made, above the level of a very low whisper, would be picked up by it [the telescreen]; moreover, so long as he remained within the field of vision which the metal plaque commanded, he could be seen as well as heard": "Always the eyes watching you . . . . working or eating, indoors or out of doors, in the bath or in bed–no escape. Nothing was your own except the few cubic centimetres inside your skull" (4 and 29).[3]

"In East Germany, the State Security agency, the Stasi, recruited possibly one sixth of the population as informers," and in Romania "Approximately seven million people, or one third of the total adult population, appeared in the Securitate's general registry already in 1965. The secret police file competed with propaganda as the largest area of state textual production, filling thousands of miles of archives" (Harper 5 and Vatulescu 6). In *The Unbearable Lightness of Being*, Milan Kundera told how Czech secret police disgraced a beloved dissident by playing tapes of his personal conversations (in which he slandered his friends) on the radio (133).

Although Orwell's satire is aimed at Soviet Russia, he "saw elements of Oceania in the England of his own days as well, not to speak of the U. S," Isaac Deutscher wrote (24-5). Britain is "the most egregious example of the surveillance society among the so-called liberal democracies. New restrictions on every aspect of life are introduced . . . almost day by day, including the controversial identity card, containing a vast amount of biometric data" (Robertson 403). England installed video surveillance systems in four major underground train stations in 1975 and began monitoring traffic flow on major highway arteries about the same time (Roberts).

America is now a state given over to extreme surveillance in the name of a god known as "national security," although this is often presented as a traumatic reaction to the shock of 9/11. And, indeed, after 9/11 a dizzying array of surveillance programs were put in place, for example., the Patriot Act of 2001 which gives the government access to our library and bookstore records or the "Anti-Terrorism Intelligence Tools Improvement Act of 2003" allowing the government to acquire any records they want and to punish anyone who threatens to expose this activity. One of these programs, ECHELON, a global surveillance system, now controlled by the U.S. National Security Agency (but started by Soviet governments in the early 1960s), is said to have the ability to intercept all phone, fax, and e-mail messages in the world.

Classic fictions of surveillance had featured actions like spying, shadowing, or tracking. Here are simple figures of watchfulness from Doyle's *The Sign of Four* and John Buchan's *The Thirty-nine Steps*:

> "It came about in this way. When the rajah put his jewels into the hands of Achmet he did it because he knew that he was a trusty man. They are suspicious folk in the East, however: so what does this rajah do but take a second even more trusty servant and set him to play the spy upon the first? This second man was ordered never to let Achmet out of his sight, and he followed him like his shadow";

and "'That is not difficult,' the Frenchman replied. 'A good spy is trained to have a photographic memory. Like your own Macaulay. You noticed he said nothing, but went through these papers again and again. I think we may assume that he has every detail stamped on his mind. When I was younger I could do the same trick'" (Doyle 151 and Buchan).

In the late twentieth and twenty-first centuries, fictions of surveillance were ratcheted up to extremes, as in Peter Weir's *The Truman Show* (1998), Tony Scott's *Enemy of the State* (1998) or Andrea Arnold's *Red Road* (2006). In the first example, Jim Carrey plays Truman Burbank, a man whose life is captured without his knowledge by 5,000 hidden cameras and broadcast live to 1.7 billion viewers as a television show. Everyone around Truman has been hired to perform the mawkish script of his life, even though Truman feels constantly uncomfortable with it. In *Enemy of the State* a tape showing a high-level governmental assassination is planted on lawyer Robert Clayton Dean (Will Smith). The NSA then cover Dean with surveillance devices and practice dirty tricks, which lead to Dean being dismissed from his job, his bank accounts frozen, and his wife throwing him out of the house. *Red Road* focuses on the massive surveillance systems deployed in the modern city, in this case Glasgow, where Jackie (Kate Dickie) works as a CCTV operator.

The surveillance in *Minority Report* (Stephen Spielberg: 2002) is even more total. In this fictional world, the speed of computers has become so rapid that it is now possible for them to predict crimes before they occur. Earlier representation of total surveillance can be found in Francis Ford Coppola's *The Conversation* (1974) where the hero, Harry Caul, is a surveillance professional assigned by the director of a large corporation to record the dialogue of a young couple who weave in and out of a lunchtime crowd in San Francisco's Union Square, and *THX-1138* (George Lucas, 1971) which portrays a society where people are drugged with sedatives and antidepressants, and have surveillance cameras watching them everywhere they go.[4]

Surveillance, Anthony Giddens reminds us, "refers to the supervisory control of subject populations, whether this control takes the form of 'visible' supervision in Foucault's sense, or the use of information to coordinate social activities" (15). And "panoptic space," Timothy Druckrey writes, "is rapidly shifting towards a post-optic one in which observation is quickly giving way to information gathering systems, databases, and the monitoring of biological and chemical agents" (151). The use of information is even more effective as an instrument of social control than visual surveillance, what Max Weber referred to as "domination through knowledge . . . the knowledge of the *file*" (Matsuda 120-

121). Before the electronic revolution such institutional surveillance had included the fingerprint system, the census, dossiers, registries, and transcripts. Later forms of social calibration continued the work of panopticism, in, for example, Taylorism (the capitalist workplace had its own Bentham, Frederick Winslow Taylor) where being measured, quantified, and written down was analogous to and more efficient than being watched.

Contemporary technology has made it possible to create extensive dossiers of extraordinary specificity about our lives, habits and tastes. Every time one uses a computer or a credit card or dials a phone (applies for a job, subscribes to a magazine, calls a mail-order catalogue, flies on a plane, buys insurance, rents an apartment, sees a doctor, borrows a book from the library, gets married or divorced–"a woman in San Francisco reported that nine months after buying a home pregnancy test from Safeway she began receiving the company's coupons for diapers and baby food, mailed to her home") one becomes part of a "data web which has proven far more powerful than the paper trails of bygone years (Parenti 100 and Sykes 2000). And the aggregate of all this information, the *database*, has great reach and power.

This aggregate can also be considered as a person's double, an informational doppelganger. Deleuze calls it a "dividual," Mark Poster a second self, Philip Agre a digital shadow (Andrejevic 2004:33). And Poster argues that the database also figures as a super-panopticon which "reconfigures the constitution of the subject": "through the database alone, the subject has been multiplied and decentered, capable of being acted upon by computers at many social locations without the least awareness by the individual concerned yet just as surely as if the individual were present somehow inside the computer" (85 and 88). The database has entered representation hyperbolically in a film like *The Net* (Irwin Winkler,1995) which is devoted to that evacuation of privacy known as "identity theft." Embedded in Ridley Scott's *Blade Runner* (1982) or Paul Verhoeven's *Total Recall* (1990) is the same as opposite, the creation of false identity through technology.

A survey of the reach of contemporary surveillance, superseded even as I write, is contained in an appendix to this chapter.

In Chaplin's *Modern Times* (1936), the president of the factory where Charlie works on the assembly line has a television-like device through which he can both spy on and communicate with his workers, and he finds Charlie trying to sneak a smoke in the bathroom. "It is now legal in all but three states," Turner writes, "for employers to place hidden cameras in locker rooms and even bathrooms . . . . And that practice is only an augmentation to timing employee phone calls, monitoring their Internet use, reading employees' email, keystroke counts, and daily tabulations of trips to the restroom" (105). "The great impresario of the mass-production assembly line, Henry Ford," wasn't content with factory surveillance; "he expected workers' 'private' lives to conform to his managerial expectations of moral probity and sent out company spies" to ensure that they did (Whitaker 38). Workplace surveillance was a prominent technology in early capitalist development: a survey conducted in 1993 found that three-quarters of large corporations "collected information about employees beyond what workers voluntarily provide. More than two-thirds reported hiring private investigators to do background checks of their workers; more than one-third . . . said they used medical records to make decisions about employees" (Sykes 1999:139).

A third field scored by intensive surveillance is the body itself. According to sociologist William Ray Arney, in the late 1940s "The organizing concept in obstetrics changed from 'confinement' to 'surveillance' . . . The hospital became the center of a system of obstetrical surveillance that extended throughout the community" (Balsamo 89). The special object of this surveillance was the pregnant female body. In an article entitled "Placing Rosemary's Baby," Sharon Marcus points out the similarities between general surveillance practices and the fetal visualization technologies of the time (amniocentesis, ultrasound imaging and fetal electrocardiograms), designed to prevent danger to the fetus from its "maternal environment" (140 and 135). Genome sciences pose a more general threat of alienating the individual from him or her self, demonstrating that they are not who they thought they were, not the children of their parents, and leading proponents of genetic privacy to demand a new right: the right not to know (Adams 204).

Does surveillance shine equally on men and women? The caption of an ad for a major Finnish department store told its women consumers, "You perform for the surveillance cameras every day. Are you dressed for it?" But women are also comforted, Hille Koskela writes, by the presence of cameras in public places as a safeguard against violence (264). In the related terrain of sexuality, one of the constant focuses of surveillance in the nineteenth and twentieth centuries was the boundary between heterosexual and homosexual.

Power, Foucault stated, is "in the hands of no one person; it's a machine in which everyone is caught, those who exercise power just as much as those over whom it is exercised" (1980:156). Surveillance can produce ambiguous or distorted results; there is a "chronic problem of error": stories circulate, for example, about incorrect names or confusion among namesakes on no-fly lists (Sykes 1999: 53). "The all-seeing surveillance camera actually depends for much of its fascination on the limitations of its gaze. The surveillance image is pored over in crime shows and pirate videos partly for the hints of what is happening off-camera, for the event obscured from view, for the distorting effects of two-dimensionality" (McGrath 78). Dörte Zbikowski writes of a blind spot in surveillance: "In order for something to be made observable at all, other things–certain fields that are ambiguously linked to observation and organize it in a certain way–drop out of the same observation" (66). "Information gleaned from surveillance practices does not necessarily produce 'knowledge'"; surveillance technology may collaborate in the reality it is theoretically there to record (Turner 109).

So the individual is not completely powerless against state or corporate surveillance; resistance is possible, although not of heroic dimensions. Foucault frequently emphasized "that where there is power there are always resistances, for power inevitably creates and works through resistance" (Lupton 22). As Sissela Bok writes of the most abject victims of surveillance, "Heads may be shaved, property and clothing removed, letters read by censors. Even in the most carefully supervised institutions, however, inmates often find a way, often through deception and secrecy, to preserve at least a modicum of privacy" (13). Foucault raised the topic in a discussion with Michelle Perrot and Jean-Pierre Barou. Perrot observed that "One feels . . . [that Bentham] has a very inadequate awareness of the degree of opacity and resistance of the material to be corrected and integrated into society–the prisoners," and Foucault commented, "almost all the eighteenth-century reformers . . . thought people would become virtuous by the simple fact of being observed" (1980:161). The eye may be all-seeing but, as in the story of Odysseus's escape from the Cyclops, it can be blinded. In the opening montage for "The Wire," (a 2002-2008 HBO series that explored the resistant relationships between the police and a vibrant drug distribution industry in a fictional Baltimore) a stone is thrown at a surveillance camera, shattering the screen. A further comment by Perrot is relevant to this brilliant television series: "These thinkers generally misunderstood the difficulty they would have in making their system take effect. They didn't realize there would always be ways of slipping through their net" (162).[5]

As sousveillance, surveillance can also empower the victims of state or economic supervision:

> in becoming a common household appliance, the small video camera transformed surveillance into a practice in which average citizens could control, rather than be controlled by, a recording gaze. A bystander's videotaping of the police beating of Rodney King in Los Angeles transformed the nature of surveillance, turning back the eye of authority upon itself . . . . *The Truman Show*, that is, only got it half right . . . we are also being encouraged to become the producers—and the ethnographers—of these virtual lives, to edit them on our iMACs even as we live them (Pecora 347-348).

Our current material culture conspires to promote personal surveillance in many ways. "Maybe Googling your date, a new acquaintance or an incoming boss wa the first step down the slippery slope of digital snooping. Now many people use Google Earth (earth.google.com) to see satellite images of a colleague's house, even the car parked in the driveway . . . . And on MySpace you can learn everything from whether a person is in a relationship, to his or her taste in music, books and friends" (Rosenbloom).

In the summer of 2000 a new type of show called "Big Brother" appeared on television; and an average of 8 to 10 million people a week watched a group of people sharing a large house, under the constant scrutiny of cameras, and thrilled as one by one they were voted off the show until only the winner remained. A later show, "Survivor," was even more popular, and "reality television" was launched on an extremely successful career. Although this trend in mass entertainment has been generally deplored, some media theorists see it as a reversal of the values that have been governing this book so far; surveillance is no longer a bad thing but rather a cure for the ills of modernity. Much earlier than this, Andrew Ross writes, to be caught in the act "by 'Candid Camera' was presented as a moment of grace. To be caught was rewarding, and not chastening, because it brought to the victim a temporary celebrity" (108).

Surveillance has changed its color and is now often regarded as a pleasure, even a virtue. The assumption behind reality TV, certainly, is that surveillance can be fun, at least for those who align themselves with the camera. But Mark Andrejevic goes further and turns it into a new folk experience: "The promise deployed by reality TV is that submission to comprehensive surveillance is not merely a character-building challenge and a 'growth' experience, but a way to participate in a medium that has long relegated audience members to the role of passive spectators" (2004:2).

However, so commentary on the subject goes, the times we live in are to blame for such prying and exhibitionism. An age of narcissism has eroded any respect of or desire for privacy. Nothing is exempt from exposure, display or exploitation; there is no remaining sense of the unspeakable--the sacred, the private. For Christopher Lasch in *The Culture of Narcissism*, contemporary American society has no emotional investment in the future, existing only for and through authenticating acts of spontaneity. "Our public sphere," Rachel Gurstein writes, is "inane and vacuous when it is not utterly mean, ugly or indecent" (4).

However, it is not so much an exhibitionist as a schizophrenic society: while polls indicate that citizens are concerned about their significant loss of privacy, the culture of exhibitionism, the voluntary offering up of our deepest and darkest privacy, still flourishes. Patricia Spacks also points to this contradiction:

> The richer we are, the more likely to seek walled enclaves for our homes and secluded Caribbean beaches for our vacations. But we watch Oprah and Geraldo, we share intimate sexual problems with pop psychologists on the radio, we consider a television appearance on *Good Morning America* a mark of success. That *we*, of course, is slippery . . . . But if *we* can designate the culture at large, my sketch suggests a set of contradictions that we all inhabit in one way or another (1998:304).

In answer to Benjamin's version of modernity in which everything shocks us, there is the contemporary cultural scene in which nothing shocks us. Censorship of obscene subject matter and expression has virtually come to an end. Is there anything any longer that cannot be shown?

> Joyce Maynard seeks to claw her way up from mediocrity by exposing her relationship with the intensely private and reclusive J. D. Salinger. Dr. Laura's ex-boyfriend sells nude pictures of the virtues maven for posting on the web. Dr. Jack Kevorkian and *60 Minutes* team up for a televised episode of euthanasia. Even the most famous privacy victims, Princess Diana and Bill Clinton, found it necessary to share details about their most intimate affairs with worldwide audiences. Privacy is worse than irrelevant (Sykes 2000).

Nothing testifies as expressively to the erosion of the border between private and public as the behavior of cell-phone users who "stride along muttering loudly to themselves, as it seems, in their private but distinctly not soundproof bubbles, oblivious to each other and their surroundings. Other people, other lives, in our ears, in our eyes, 'in your face': there is just so much now we don't want to know" (Poole 79).

In1870, novelist Richard Grant White noted that some society people furnished journalists with guest lists and descriptions of private parties: "I am inclined to believe that some people think that no pleasure is fully enjoyed until an account of it is published" (Gurstein 38). In her book, Deborah Nelson revisited "the extravagant self-disclosure" of American confessional poets of the mid twentieth century--Anne Sexton, Robert Lowell, Sylvia Plath, John Berryman and W. D. Snodgrass--censured at the time for their "socially shameful disclosures" of family secrets–insanity, divorce, sex and alcoholism (xiv-xv and 30). In 1959 Norman Mailer publishes *Advertisements for Myself.*

Bromwich argues that publicity is now regarded as an authenticating experience, that many people do not feel real uil they have been "published": "Publicity, as I use the term," refers to the "process, a rite of passage now conducted by American society in a great many venues, by which we are solicited to recognize ourselves and to know ourselves most alive as an image . . . . Its success depends on the puzzling fact that the irrevocable passage from depth to surface can be experienced as a relief" (a.146-147). Selah Tarrant in James' *The Bostonians* feels that the truly happy people were those "of whom there was some journalistic mention every day of the year": his "ideal of bliss was to be as regularly and indispensably a component part of the newspaper as the title and the date" (1985:895). Nathanael West's Miss Lonelyhearts comes to know "that for the tear-soaked and the traumatized who write to ask his advice, the public working through of their misery from a low to a lower depth is its own reward. It is more real to them than the life to which they would return if their letters ever had to stop" (Bromwich b.155). The other side of this topic is the way in which publication delivers one up to their "public": in Louisa May Alcott's *Jo's Boys*, Jo learns that she is no longer her own woman:

> for suddenly the admiring public took possession of her and all her affairs . . . . If she declined to open her heart to them, they

> reproached her . . . . and if she preferred the privacy of home to the pedestal upon which she was requested to pose, 'the airs of literary people' were freely criticized," As a popular author, Jo has become public property. Readers arrive daily to claim her time, her history, even her "heart." But metafictional irony and ambivalence aside, Alcott, after all, made a hugely profitable career of marketing herself. The marketing of authorial privacy was not uncommon in nineteenth-century America (Adams 159).

The self is more real as a representation than in the "flesh." "I heard a noncelebrity guest on *Oprah Winfrey* confide to Oprah that she had never told her best friends what she was about to say . . . . Why was she telling the camera now? At this point the usual instruments of moral psychology are at a loss . . . . All this occurs in a haze of euphoria that is the very element of the media" (Bromwich b.146).

What has been lost or abandoned in our age are inhibition, repression, shame (to name it negatively) and (positively) tact, reticence, discretion, diplomacy. Were they only the fading remnants of Victorianism or were they proper identity barriers? Or were they the armor of privilege for a masculine middle class? Jean Baudrillard has argued that what has disappeared in this postmodern age is privacy itself, private space in which the subject can establish a sense of interiority (1983:130-131).

Various causes are offered for this affective apocalypse, such as the 1960s with its ethos of "letting it all hang out." Great cultural shifts occurred in America in the sixties when narcissism became the national pastime. The cultural turn is also blamed on the middle-class penchant for therapy where "Americans share their intimacies and dysfunctions with therapists, casual acquaintances, and national television audiences . . . . Keeping one's dysfunction or family turmoil to oneself is not only regarded as suspicious but potentially unhealthy" (Sykes 6 and168).

And yet is this really new? Wasn't it always like this?. Jane Austen describes something like it in *Northanger Abbey*, when she has Henry Tilney remind Catherine Moreland, "Remember the country and the age in which we live

. . . . where social and literary intercourse is on such a footing; where every man is surrounded by a neighborhood of voluntary spies, and where roads and papers lay every thing open" (2004:136). "But now all is to be changed . . . . All the decent drapery of life is to be rudely torn off. All the superadded ideas, furnished from the wardrobe of a moral imagination, which the heart owns, and the understanding ratifies, as necessary to cover the defects of our naked shivering nature, and to raise it to dignity in our own estimation, are to be exploded as a ridiculous, absurd, and antiquated fashion," so wrote Edmund Burke in 1790 in his "Reflections on the Revolution in France" (66). Isn't every age accused of narcissism by its fading generations? Coleridge called the early nineteenth century "this age of personality, this age of literary and political gossiping . . . a generation so transformed from the characteristic reserve of Britons, that from the ephemeral sheet of a London newspaper, to the everlasting Scotch professorial quarto, almost every publication exhibits or flatters the epidemic distemper [of memoir and confession]" (178). When Maria Edgeworth refused to let John Gibson Lockhart print her letters from Sir Walter Scott, she wrote:

> The general rage for the practice upheld by venality and vanity leagued together on one hand and depraved curiosity and malice on the other threatens to destroy private friendship and all human confidence and leave no *privacy* in this world, no *true* feeling– Every high or delicate sentiment which in their very natures cannot bear display are now dragged to light–blasted, withered by the horrid, garish eye of curiosity" (Hart 308).

APPENDIX

Recent books and articles have reported on a staggering array of surveillance agencies and the new engines that allow them to do their work:

- a variety of scanning devices: surveillance cameras (in the U. K. there is one camera for every 14 people); "Keyhole-class" satellites which can distinguish an object as small as five or six inches large on the ground; "Human Identification at a Distance" developed technologies that are capable of identifying a person at up to 500 feet by their facial features; "Forward Looking InfraRed" which detects even the tiniest difference in temperature and enables its user to detect what is happening inside buildings; biometric scans (fingerprints, DNA, facial patterns, manner of walking, or voice); and "smart cards" (Sykes 1999:37 and 41). "The AGEMA System," Turner writes, "is an imaging device that can peer into houses from the street (or from helicopters above) by discriminating heat ratios . . . . . And pilotless drones are now being developed by the military to provide airborne surveillance. These miniature camera-equipped drones are being engineered as minuscule, quiet, remotely- piloted vehicles the size of a wasp" (105).
- monitoring programs for phone conversations and internet activity (including social networks): Federal law enforcement agencies under the Communications Assistance For Law Enforcement Act (1994) aided by systems such as Carnivore (1997), NarusInsight (2005), ECHELON (late 1980s), TEMPEST (late 1960s), "Hancock" (2001), "Magic Lantern" (2001) and CIPAV (2011), utilizing, for telephones, speech-to-text software and, for the internet, automated surveillance computers which sift through the vast amount of intercepted traffic identifying "trigger" words or phrases (Wiki, "Surveillance");
- vast databases--"Pinwale" (2005); the Defense Advanced Research Project's Agency's Information Awareness Office administers a program known as "Total Information Awareness" (TIA) (2002) which is designed to gather data from all available intelligence sources and compile it into a mammoth database– and programs to search and communicate among the various databases (automated video analysis software [such as VIRAT (2008) and HumanID] (2002)]) (Wiki, "Surveillance").
- Profiling programs: ADVISE and TALON.

The organizations and powers to carry out this surveillance are vested in the U. S. Department of Homeland Security, the largest reorganization of government in over half a century: a domestic intelligence agency of labyrinthine complexity involving more than 170,000 new employees and unprecedented organizational mandates (Richard Garrard).

NOTES

Privacy and the private

1. In answer to the question of what in the interior mix is actually private, Warren and Brandeis claimed that they were not intending to protect the expression, thoughts and feelings involved, but rather the peace of mind which such protection affords (200).

2. Nietzsche identifies these two forces (Hoy 129).

3. The sanctity of the self may have been a modulation of an earlier sanctity of the soul, but it was also implicit in John Locke's claim that we own ourselves: "Every man has a property in his own person" (1952:16). The sanctity of life, however, is a twentieth-century Catholic doctrine declaring that we have no right to end our own or another's life because it is owned by God (i.e. made in the image of God).

4. Barrington Moore claims that "By the third century BC and probably much earlier, Chinese thinkers had developed a sharp distinction between the concepts of public and private," while Deborah Pellow counters or explains this: "In traditional Chinese, there is no character for the word *privacy* . . . . Just prior to the unification of China in the third century BC, the philosopher Han Fei Tzu regarded private behavior as potentially subversive . . . . [But] even in ancient China there was a sense of privacy . . . . But it was privacy for the intimate group" (Moore 221 and Pellow 34).

5. Lena Orlin balances this generalization with its opposite:

> Privacy is usually associated with the Reformation emphases on direct engagement with scripture, self-examination, and personal

> accountability for spirituality. At the same time, however, the Reformation was responsible for important deprivatizations of moral experience [religious courts examining into transgressions, the pillory] . . . . In this way the Reformation worked to stimulate the flow of information about personal and family matters (10).

6. The legal stress seems ironic against the background of the doctrine as expressed here by E. L. Godkin, founding editor of the *Nation*: in disputes about property, "people were generally willing to relegate their claims for justice to the state; but when it came to matters of personal insult . . . 'there is certain peculiar fitness in protecting reputation or privacy against libel or intrusion by the cudgel or the horsewhip.'" Legal redress may have some value but not for privacy: it "only makes matters worse by the publication of everything sacred to your privacy, conjoined with a detestable notoriety and the expense of a wearisome litigation" (Gurstein 37 and 155).

7. Another privacy right articulated by the Supreme Court in 1957 and 1966 was the right to remain silent.

8. "As a French article warns visitors to the United States, America is a place where "strangers suddenly share information with you about their 'private activities' in a way that is 'difficult to imagine' for northern Europeans or Asians" and "Americans have a particularly embarrassing habit, continental Europeans believe, of talking about salaries. It is 'normal in America,' an Internet site informs German tourists, for your host at dinner to ask 'not just how much you earn, but even what your net worth is'"-- topics ordinarily quite off-limits under the rules of European etiquette. On the other hand, "Americans are puzzled by the ill-bred way in which Europeans casually take off their clothes . . . . What kind of 'privacy' is there, Americans will ask, in countries where people prance around naked out of doors while allowing the state to keep tabs on their whereabouts, convict them on the basis of unfair police investigations, peer into their living rooms, tap their phones, and even dictate what names they can give to their babies?" (Whitman 1155 and 1158-1159). That European reticence, however, was observed in the U. S. too when I was young and changed about the time that everyone started calling me by my first name.

9. The paradox operates in the visual arts as well. One of the conditions for Godiva's ride is that the inhabitants of the town keep their shutters closed. No one sees her naked on a horse except Peeping Tom, who is later blinded for his sin. yet "art, sculpture, and poetry have never tired of showing Godiva's naked female body in representations of her ride, imitating the position of Peeping Tom" (Kelly 223).

10, Like other knots in this book, this one is contested: for example, Mary Crane insists that enclosed space outside the house afforded more privacy than interior space. Architecture also worked in an opposite direction to dissolve intimate domestic space: Sharon Marcus notes "how Parisian apartment-house façades of the Restoration period aspired to an ideal of visual transparency--achieved through increased use of windows and simplified ornamentation" (Gaylin 61). The central observation of Betsy Klimasmith's *At Home in the City* is that "the boundedness of the rural home gave way to an urban domesticity, where home is understood in terms of permeability, interconnectedness, and the fluidity of private and public spaces" (Bramen 1266).

11. The trope of bucolic retreat had been around since classical antiquity, but in eighteenth-century America it was fulsomely endorsed: by William Penn--"The country life is to be preferred . . . a sweet and natural retreat from noise and talk . . . [that] allows opportunity for reflection"--and George Washington: "under the shadow of my own vine and my own fig tree. Free from the bustle of a camp and the busy scenes of public life, I am solacing myself with those tranquil enjoyments . . . . I am not only retired from all public employments, but I am retiring within myself" (Robert Smith 17 and 31).

12. The irrationalities of privacy weighed upon Charlotte Perkins Gilman and Frances Trollope. The first declared the concern for privacy absurd since Americans allowed their home to be "vulgarly invaded by low-class strangers": We introduce into our homes "Strangers by birth, by class, by race, by education—as utterly alien as it is possible to conceive . . . [into] our very bed chambers; in knowledge of all the daily habits of our lives—and then we talk of privacy!" (Mattis 290). Trollope made similar objections to a southern woman "lacing her stays with the most perfect composure before a Negro footman" (Goffman 123). To the protagonist of Algernon Blackwood's *A Prisoner in Fairyland*, "the very idea of servants was . . . an affliction; he loathed their prying closeness to his intimate life and habits, destroying the privacy he loved."

13. It's not simply a matter of the government withholding or lying. In the exhausted public sphere, everybody lies (only the government lies twice as much and twice as big), no party can afford not to. Publication is an entry in a liars' club, so, for example, in estimating the size of a protest, one assumes that the public public low estimate is wildly inaccurate and the low private public (that of the protesters themselves) only mildly so.

The private and the public

1. Engaged fiction, for example, whether Communist or post-colonial, always runs this risk of being neutralized by privatizing signs of creativity, stylization or pleasure as reviews of Zora Neale Hurston's *Their Eyes Were Watching God* or Maxine Hong Kingston's *The Woman Warrior* show (Sanborn 1334).

2. In addition, even though the public and the private have traditionally been seen as opposed or at least diverse realms, they have also been treated as analogical sites (the public king and the private father) and sometimes they become metaphors for one another.

3. The various distinctions are "neither mutually reducible nor wholly unrelated . . . . [They] do not simply point to different phenomena; often they rest on different underlying images of the social world, are driven by different concerns, generate different problematics, and raise very different issues" (Weintraub 2).

4. Women of color tended to enter the public sphere in the private sphere of white women. The ironies of public and private in gay life are many. The U. S. Supreme Court had outed gays long before magazines and blogs did, in the 1986 ruling *Bowers v. Hardwick*.

> Hardwick and his male sex-partner may have believed that Hardwick's bedroom was a private location and that the presumption of privacy offered them some protection from the state of Georgia's prohibitions against practicing sodomy. The Court ruled, however, that while such a right to privacy certainly holds in instances of (heterosexual) marriage, family and procreation, "none of [those] rights bears any resemblance" to a sexual privacy right–at least for homosexuals (Leap 9).

Gay people have usually had to find privacy in public space, like the coin-operated stall in a public washroom.

5. "At the same time people lament a loss of privacy," Nancy Welch writes,

> millions of Americans live in 5,000-plus square-foot homes in gated communities . . . . Since the 1980s companies have increasingly asserted a "corporate right to privacy" . . . to justify a growing use of confidentiality agreements in the settlement of sexual harassments, workplace discrimination and products liability lawsuits . . . . The agents of neoliberalism such as the International Monetary Fund have made privatization a key condition for any country seeking economic aid (20).

6. Consider also Sir Francis Bacon and Emerson: ". . . it is a theme so common to extol a private life, not taxed with sensuality and sloth, in comparison and to the disadvantage of a civil life, for safety, liberty, pleasure, and dignity, or at least freedom from indignity"; and

> In history our imagination plays us false [insofar as it repeatedly tells us that] . . . . Kingdom and lordship, power and estate, are a gaudier vocabulary than private John and Edward in a small house and common day's work; but the things of life are the same to both; the sum total of both is the same. Why all this deference to Alfred and Scanderbeg and Gustavus? Suppose they were virtuous; did they wear out virtue? As great a stake depends on your private act to-day, as followed their public and renowned steps (Bacon and Emerson 1950:154-155).

7. Even more, for Walter Benjamin, this distinction became the larger one between fantasy or illusion and reality: "For the private individual . . . . [the interior of his dwelling] represents the universe. In the interior he brings together the far away and the long ago. His living room is a box in the theater of the world" (1999:8-9).

8.

> Then he drew her towards him, and in a moment she was kneeling at his feet, with her face buried on his knees. Considering their ages perhaps we must say that their attitude was awkward. They would certainly have thought so themselves had they imagined that any one could have seen them. But how many absurdities of the kind are not only held to be pleasant, but almost holy (Trollope 816-817).

9. In an article on the Jamesian child, Maeve Pearson points to the ironic interchange of public and private in the fiction where the private space "most subject to invidious intrusion in his stories is the nursery" (107).

10. Margery Sabin presents an interesting variation on this topic in the form of "language selves," in the cases of two writers, Richard Rodriguez and Eva Hoffman, who lost the use of their native language through immigration. Rodriguez insists that his was a fortunate fall:

> . . . the English language, he argues, allowed him to attain the public identity in the American community that confinement in

> Spanish would have prohibited. Yet Rodriguez acknowledges the huge cost to this private self in this achievement . . . . Hoffman recalls her migration . . . to the English language as an exile, not only from a particular cultural milieu, but from her own most private sense of self: "What has happened to me in this new world . . . . I'm not filled with language anymore, and I have only a memory of fullness to anguish me with the knowledge that, in this dark and empty state, I don't really exist" (289-290).

11. Even the public of Walter Lippmann (1922) was admittedly phantasmal: "Modern society is not visible to anybody, nor intelligible continuously and as a whole. One section of it is visible to another section, one series of acts is intelligible to this group and another to that" (Robbins ix).

12. "The second notion of 'public' is the one we have in mind if we speak of Mediterranean . . . cities having a rich public life. It is what Philippe Ariès means when he says that, in the society of the old regime, 'life . . . was lived in public.' The key to . . . [this public] is not solidarity or obligation but sociability . . . . The citizens who 'rush' to the public space of the assembly do so to engage in self-conscious collective action, deliberation, and decision concerning common–that is, 'public'–affairs. When we venture into Jane Jacobs' public space, on the other hand, we enter what Roger Scruton has aptly termed 'a sphere of broad and largely unplanned encounter,' of fluid sociability among strangers and near-strangers" (Weintraub 17-18).

Invasions of privacy: surveillance and voyeurism

1. Not only is *Moby Dick* a Romantic critique of analytic philosophy, it is a critique of Romantic philosophy as well, in particular, the Kantian/Hegelian search for the *ding an sich.* The chapter "The Whiteness of the Whale" is a wonderful analogy to the quest for essence: it is a circumnavigation of the whale that gradually strips him of all dispensible predicates and connotations. Unpredicate whatever can be predicated and whatever remains is the elusive essence. Ishmael circumnavigates the whale philosophically: he sails up through its positive qualities and back down again stripping it of negatives. He achieves ever purer whiteness until at the finale he is looking at whiteness itself, a field that is so intense, I would argue, that he goes blind and the white universe turns black.

A counterpart to this chapter and the whiteness of truth can be found in Ishmael's ruminations on the black painting just inside the Spouter Inn. Gazing breeds compulsion, and, after looking for a while, Ishmael takes an oath with himself "to find out what that marvelous painting meant." The painting offers "Such unaccountable masses of shades and shadows, that at first you almost thought some ambitious young artist . . . had endeavored to delineate chaos bewitched . . . . what most puzzled and confounded you was a long, limber, portentous, black mass of something hovering in the centre of the picture . . . Yet was there a sort of indefinite, half-attained, unimaginable sublimity about it that fairly froze you to it" (1983:805). And, of course, he finds what he expects: Moby-Dick, at the center of everything.

2. Not merely words but even gestures could arouse suspicion (or even a back, "even a back can be revealing," Winston thought): "a nervous tic, an unconscious look of anxiety, a habit of muttering to yourself--anything that carried with it the suggestion of abnormality, of having something to hide. In any case, to wear an improper expression on your face (to look incredulous when a victory was announced, for example) was a punishable offense. There was even a word for it ...: *facecrime*, it was called": "Your worst enemy, he reflected, was your own nervous system. At any moment the tension inside you was liable to translate itself into some visible symptom" (Orwell 5, 65 and 67).

3. The modern revision of the male gaze begins, all agree, with the appearance in Sartre's 1945 work, *Being and Nothingness*, of a long chapter on the look (*le regard*). Sartre destabilized Descartes' longstanding formulation of knowledge as disinterested looking that results in owning the object one is looking at. In Sartre "The Cartesian self-reflecting *cogito* is replaced by a self that is constituted by the gaze of the other" (Jay 288). Looking always elicits a responsive gaze which can reduce the subject to shame because the observer realizes that the world is full of other subjects all looking at something, possibly him: "The gaze of the other objectifies me, petrifies me, degrades me, disintegrates my universe, alienates me from my possibilities and strips me of my transcendence" (Lacoste 44). In Lacan's later work the gaze casts a wider net and refers to the sense that the object of our eye's look "is somehow looking back at us of its own will. This uncanny feeling of being gazed at by the object of our look affects us in the same way as castration anxiety . . . . We may believe that we are in control of our eye's look; however, any feeling of scopophilic power is eventually undone" (Felluga).

4. In Melville, the sadistic gaze is an attribute possessed by Jackson in *Redburn* ("One glance of his squinting eye was as good as a knock-down, for it was the most deep, subtle, infernal looking eye, that I ever saw lodged in a human head") and Ahab ("As the unsetting polar star, which through the livelong, arctic, six months' night sustains its piercing, steady, central gaze; so Ahab's purpose now fixedly gleamed down upon the constant midnight of the gloomy crew. It

domineered above them so, that all their bodings, doubts, misgivings, fears, were fain to hide beneath their souls") (1983:67 and 1365).

5. This distinction is put to work in Poe's *Narrative of Arthur Gordon Pym*, when Pym, trapped in the hold of a ship, tries, in the dark, to read a note that his friend Augustus has sent him, tied to the dog Tiger's neck: "The white slip of paper could barely be discerned, and not even that when I looked at it directly; by turning the exterior portions of the retina towards it, that is to say, by surveying it slightly askance, I found that it became in some measure perceptible" (1984b:1032-1033). Cf Thoreau: "Sometimes I would rather get a transient glimpse or side view of a thing than stand fronting to it . . . . The object I caught a glimpse of as I went by haunts my thoughts a long time, is infinitely suggestive, and I do not care to front it and scrutinize it" (1906:164).

6. Surveillance "reverses the principle of the dungeon, or rather of its three functions--to enclose, to deprive of light and to hide (Foucault 1977:200).

7. The author who best represents the shift from disciplinary society to societies of control is William Burroughs (James Phillips).

8. Miller also devotes a little space to the continental novel: Stendhal's *The Red and the Black*, where "Constant supervision is secured either by the Abbé Castanède's secret police or through Abbé Pirard's 'moyen de surveillance,'" and Balzac (19).

9. Crusoe spends much time and energy building walls around himself. He prefers enclosures without doors, and he describes several designs which allow him to pull his door in after him. His response to the sighting of the footprint and the cannibal feast is to eliminate all signs of himself: "In this extremity I went back directly to my castle, pulled up the ladder after me, and made all things without look as wild and natural as I could. . . . not to leave the least sign for them to guess by that there were any living creatures upon the island--I mean of human shape." He further decides "to throw down my enclosures and turn all my tame cattle wild . . . digging up my two corn fields . . . that they might not see any vestiges of habitation, and be prompted to look farther."

What follows is an utterly fantastic episode in which Crusoe literally goes to ground. Behind a thick branch of low brushwood, he discovers a hollow place. In this new apartment, he finds, to his unspeakable consolation, "a mere natural cave in the earth, which went in a vast way, and where, I daresay, no savage . . . would be so hardy as to venture in." When totally self-effaced, he has an unparalleled moment of content in an otherwise anxious narrative: "I could have been content to have capitulated for spending the rest of my time there, even to the last moment, till I had laid me down and died."

10. Shamir reads "Wakefield" very differently: "he has found a way to create within marriage a space of interior privacy by installing himself as an absent presence in his home." And she likens this fiction to the historical moment when the middle-class, urban male began to leave his home daily to go to work, thereby, indeed, "withdrawing into a state of absent presence within the domestic sphere" (Shamir 2006:73).

11. Even before the development of detective fiction, the surveillant anxiety of fiction had become manifest in the emergence of "realism": "'To see' is the dominant verb in the realist text--'la gastronomie de l'oeil' as Balzac expressed it'--and realist fiction is preeminently concerned with seeing, with a seeing in detail." Emerson, in his *English Traits*, had noted of Swift, "He describes his fictitious persons as if for the police," and Zola had declared that "We novelists are the examining magistrates of men and their passions" (Seltzer 50-51).

12. Hawthorne borrowed this trope wholesale from the French author Alain-René Lesage. The narrator of Dickens' *Dombey and Son*, expresses the same wish out of ostensibly moral desires, and, at the end of the century, Arthur Conan Doyle in "A Case of Identity," would also wish to "fly out of that window hand in hand, hover over this great city, gently remove the roofs, and peep in at the queer things which are going on, the strange coincidences, the plannings, the cross-purposes, the wonderful chains of events, working through generations, and leading to the most *outré* results" (190).

13. Moments of peeping or sly looking are central to many of Hawthorne's tales as well, notably "Roger Malvin's Funeral," "The Maypole of Merrymount" and "Young Goodman Brown." The opening of *The Scarlet Letter* is a sustained look at a woman's engorged breasts by the entire village under the feint that something of great moral import is written there. In the *Marble Faun* an evil spirit, the Mephistopheles of Art Galleries, attempts to reduce all art-looking to pornographic voyeurism, thus reversing Freud's exemption of erotic visual lingering which, he said, belongs to the more sublimated realms of culture (Bronfen 60).

14. In addition to the domestic surveillance manifest in the film, Robert J. Corber argues for an alignment of Jeff's activities with those of the newly formed national security state (83-110).

The erosion of privacy

1. Turner goes on to sketch the state of "omnivideo" in which we currently live: "An infestation of stationary cameras stare at us as we browse through Borders and Barnes & Noble, at Blockbuster, SuperAmerica, and every ATM machine worldwide (themselves already interconnected to financial surveillance apparatuses) . . . . These cameras peer from skyscrapers 'with lenses that can count the buttons on a blouse three miles away'" (102-103).

2. For example, the Privacy Act of 1974 which was "a response to privacy concerns raised by Watergate-era abuses"; the Foreign Intelligence Surveillance Act of 1978 which attempted to regulate wiretapping in national security cases; and the Electronic Communications Privacy Act of 1986 (Berman 312).

3, The telescreen receives and transmits simultaneously: "Every citizen or at least every citizen important enough to be worth watching, could be kept for twenty-four hours a day under the eyes of the police and in the sound of official propaganda, with all other channels of communication closed" (214). In addition there is the Police Patrol, "snooping into people's windows" (4). In Yevgeny Zamyatin's *We*, an important source for Orwell, the members of One State "live in glass enclosures where everyone can watch each other as no citizen has anything to hide . . . . [They] are allowed to 'lower their shades' during prescribed and pre-approved Sexual days when they are entitled to have sexual relations with anyone they wish as long as they notify the government." The surveillants are the "Guardians" who dress like everyone else and meld into the general population. In addition, special "membranes" (listening devices) are mounted on all the streets (Giridarin).

4.

> . . . technologies of simulation are forms of *hypersurveillant control*, where the prefix "hyper" implies not simply an intensification of surveillance, but the effort to push surveillance techniques to their absolute limit. That limit is an imaginary line beyond which control operates, so to speak, in "advance" of itself. . . . Simulation technology . . . is part of . . . the *imaginary* of surveillance control–a fantastic dream of seeing everything capable of being seen, recording every fact capable of being recorded, and accomplishing these things whenever and wherever possible, prior to the event itself (Bogard 4-5).

5. Another path of resistance to surveillance is paved by paranoia, which is "a necessary product of all information systems" (Bersani 103). Paranoia is both the cover under which the facts of surveillance are displaced and, in the form of "adequate paranoia" (or "paranoia within reason" as George Marcus termed it, or the American Psychiatry Association's "healthy paranoia") a safeguard for the stability of the self (Holm 39).

WORKS CITED

Adams, Katherine. *Owning Up: Privacy, Property, and Belonging in U. S. Women's Life Writing*. NY: Oxford UP, 2009.

Addison, Joseph and Richard Steele. *The Spectator*. http://www.gutenberg.org/files/12030/12030-h/12030-h/12030-h.htm.

Ainley, Rosa. *New Frontiers of Space, Bodies and Gender*. NY: Routledge, 1998.

Alcott, Bronson. *Orphic Sayings*.

Althusser, Louis. "Ideology and Ideological State Apparatuses." *Lenin and Philosophy*. NY: Monthly Review Press, 1969.

"Anarchist Without Content." "The Rise of the Social." http://anarchistwithoutcontent.wordpress.com/2011/02/24/the-rise-of-the-social/.

Andrejevic, Mark. *Ispy: Surveillance and Power in the Interactive Era*. Lawrence: University Press of Kansas, *2007*.

________. *Reality TV: The Work of Being Watched*. NY: Rowman & Littlefield Publishers, Inc., 2004.

Apter, Emily. "What Is Yours, Ours and Mine: Authorial Ownership and the Creative Commons." *October* #126, Fall 2008, 91-114.

Arendt, Hannah. *The Human Condition*. University of Chicago Press, 1958.

________. *Origins of Totalitarianism*. NY: Schocken Books, 2004.

Ariès, Philippe. "Introduction." 1-12. In *Passions of the Renaissance. A History of Private Life*. Edited by Roger Chartier. Cambridge, Mass.: Belknap Press of Harvard University Press, 1989. Volume III.

Aristotle. *The Complete Works: The Revised Oxford Translation*. Edited by Jonathan Barnes. Princeton UP, 1995.

Austen, Jane. *Northanger Abbey*. NY: W. W. Norton & Company, 2004.

________. *Persuasion*. Petersborough, ON: Broadview Press, 1998.

Ayer, A. J. "Could Language Be Invented by a Robinson Crusoe?" 53-55. In *The Private Language Argument*. Edited by O. R. Jones. London: Macmillan, 1971.

Bacon Francis. *The Advancement of Learning*. http://www.gutenberg.org/dirs/etext04/adlr10h.htm.

Bagehot, Water. "Shakespeare The Man." *Literary Studies*. NY: Dutton, 1911.

Bakhtin, Mikhail. *Problems of Dostoevsky's Poetics*. Minneapolis: University of Minnesota Press, 1984.

Balsamo, Anne Marie. *Technologies of the Gendered Body: Reading Cyborg Women*. Duke UP. 1996.

Balzac, Honoré de. *Bureaucracy*. http://www.gutenberg.org/files/1343/1343-h/1343-h.htm.

Barker, Francis. *The Tremulous Private Body: Essays on Subjection*. NY: Methuen, 1984.

Barrie, J. M. *Alice-Sit-By-the-Fire*. NY: Charles Scribner's Sons, 1930.

Barthes, Roland. *Camera Lucida: Reflections on Photography*. NY: Hill and Wang, 1981.

_________. *S/Z*. NY: Hill and Wang, 1974.

Bartolovich, Crystal. "Inventing London." 13-40. In *Masses, Classes, and the Public Sphere*. Edited by Mike Hill, Warren Montag and Crystal Bartolovich. NY: Verso, 2000.

Baudrillard, Jean. "Ecstasy of Communication." 126-134. In *The Anti-Aesthetic*. Edited by Hal Foster. Port Townsend, WA: Bay Press, 1983.

________. *The Intelligence of Evil or the Lucidity Pact*. NY: Berg, 2005.

Bauman, Zygmunt. *Identity: Conversations with Bendetto Vecchi*. Cambridge: Polity Press, 2004.

Benjamin, Walter. *The Arcades Project*. Cambridge: Harvard UP, 1999.

________. "The Work of Art in the Age of Mechanical Reproduction." 219-254. *Illuminations*. NY: Harcourt, Brace & World, 1955.

Berger, John. *Ways Of Seeing*. NY: Penguin, 2008.

Bergman, Jill and Debra Bernardi, editors. *Our Sisters' Keepers: Nineteenth-century Benevolence Literature by American Women*. Tuscaloosa: University of Alabama Press, 2005.

Berlant, Laurent. "Intimacy: A Special Issue." *Critical Inquiry* 24(2), 1998, 281-288.

Berman, Jerry and Paula Bruening. "Is Privacy Still Possible in the Twenty-first Century?" *Social Research* 68(1), 2001, 306-318.

Bersani, Leo. "Pynchon, Paranoia and Literature." *Representations* 25, 1989, 99-118.

Bisla, Sundeep. "The Return of the Author: Privacy, Publication, the Mystery Novel, and *The Moonstone*." *boundary 2* 29(1), 2002, 177-222.

Blackwood, Algernon. *A Prisoner in Fairyland.* http://www.gutenberg.org/cache/epub/6021/pg6021.html.

Blumenberg, Hans. *The Legitimacy of the Modern Age*. Cambridge, MA: MIT Press, 1983.

Bogard, William. *Simulation of Surveillance: Hypercontrol in Telematic Societies*. NY: Cambridge UP, 1996.

Bok, Sissela. *Secrets: On the Ethics of Concealment and Revelation*. NY: Vintage Books, 1989.

Boling. Patricia. *Privacy and the Politics of Intimate Life*. Ithaca: Cornell UP, 1996.

Braddon, Mary Elizabeth. *Aurora Floyd*. NY: Oxford UP, 1996.

Bramen, Carrie Tirado. "At Home in the City." *Journal of American History* 93(4), 2005, 1266.

Brand, Dana. *The Spectator and the City in Nineteenth-century American Literature*. NY: Cambridge UP, 1991.

Brewer, John. "This, that and the other: Public, Social and Private in the Seventeenth and Eighteenth Centuries." 1-21. In *Shifting the Boundaries*. Edited by Dario Castiglione and Lesley Sharpe. University of Exeter Press, 1995.

Brighenti, Andrea Mubi. "Surveillance and the Visual." *Surveillance & Society* 5(2), 2008, 209-216.

Brodhead, Richard H. "Veiled Ladies: Toward a History of Antebellum Entertainment." *American Literary History* 1(2), 1989, 273-294 .

Bromwich, David. Bromwich, a. "How Publicity Makes People Real." *Social Research* 68(1), 2001, 145-172.

________. b. "Introduction." *Social Research* 68(1), p. 1.

Bronfen, Elizabeth, "Killing Gazes, Killing in the Gaze: On Michael Powell's *Peeping Tom*." 59-89. In *Gaze and Voice as Love Objects*. Edited by Renata Salecl and Slavoj Žižek. Durham: Duke UP, 1996.

Bronte, Charlotte. *Villette*. Oxford: Clarendon Press, 1984.

Brooks, Peter. *Body Work: Objects of Desire in Modern Narrative*. Cambridge: Harvard UP, 1993.

Brown, Gillian. *Domestic Individualism: Imagining Self in Nineteenth-century America*. Berkeley: University of California Press, 1990.

Bryant, Christopher G. A. "Privacy, Privatization and Self-Determination." 59-86. In Young.

Buchan, John. *The Thirty-nine Steps*. http://www.gutenberg.org/ebooks/558.

Burke, Edmund. "Reflections on the Revolution in France." New Haven: Yale UP, 2003.

__________. "A Philosophical Inquiry into the Origin of our Ideas of the Sublime and Beautiful. " http://www.gutenberg.org/files/15043/15043-h/15043-h.htm.

Burke, Peter. "Representations of the Self From Petrarch to Descartes." 17-28. In Porter.

Burney, Fanny *The Diary and Letters of Madame D'Arblay*, Volume 1. http://www.gutenberg.org/cache/epub/5826/pg5826.html.

Butler, Judith. "Performative Acts and Gender Constitution: An Essay in Phenomenology and Feminist Theory." *Performing Feminisms: Feminist Critical Theory and Theatre*. Edited by Sue-Ellen Case. Baltimore: Johns Hopkins UP, 1990.

Calvert, Clay. *Voyeur Nation: Media, Privacy, and Peering in Modern Culture*. Boulder, Colo.: Westview Press, 2000.

Chabot, Steven. "Subject/Object." http://subjectobject.net/2007/02/21/sociologist-richard-sennett-and- the-public-life-of-the-internet/.

Chase, Karen and Michael Levenson. *The Spectacle of Intimacy*. Princeton UP, 2000.

Chlopecki, Mary. "The Property Rights Origins of Privacy Rights." *The Freeman*, April 23, 2012.

Cho, K. Daniel. "Curiosity According to Psychoanalysis: Blumenberg, Freud, and the Destiny of an Affect." *New German Critique* 35(2), 2008, 191-2005.

Cieraad, Irene, editor. *At Home: An Anthropology of Domestic Space*. Syracuse UP, 1999.

Cohn, Dorrit. "Optics and Power in the Novel." *New Literary History* 26(1), 1995, 3-20.

Coleridge, Samuel Taylor. *Biographia Literaria*. 155-482. *Major Works*. Edited by H. J. Jackson. NY: Oxford UP, 2000.

Collins, Wilkie. *The Woman in White*. Peterborough, ON: Broadview Press, 2006.

Collings, David. *Monstrous Society: Reciprocity, Discipline, and the Political Uncanny, c. 1740-1848*. Lewisburg: Bucknell UP, 2009.

Colomina, Beatriz. *Privacy and Publicity: Modern Architecture as Mass Media.* Cambridge, MA: MIT Press, 1994.

Constant, Benjamin. *Prophecy From the Past: Benjamin Constant on Conquest and Usurpation.* NY: Reynal & Hitchcock, 1941.

Cooper, James Fenimore. *The Prairie.* Albany: SUNY Press, 1985.

Corber, Robert J. *In the Name of National Security: Hitchcock, Homophobia, and the Political Construction of Gender in Postwar America.* Durham: Duke UP, 1993..

Cott, Nancy. "Privacy." 540-543. In *A Companion to American Thought.* Edited by Richard Wightman Fox and James T. Kloppenberg. Oxford: Blackwell, 1995.

Couldry, Nick. *Why Voice Matters: Culture and Politics After Neoliberalism.* London: Sage, 2010.

Cranch, Christopher. "Gnosis."

http://www.theotherpages.org/poems/cranch01.html.

Crane, Mary Thomas. "Illicit Privacy and Outdoor Spaces in Early Modern England." *Journal for Early Modern Cultural Studies* 9(1), 2009, 4-22.

Croce, Benedetto. *Breviary of Aesthetics.* Indianapolis: Hackett Pub. Co, 1995.

Cubitt, Sean. "The difference between privacy and anonymity." [2002] http://permalink.gmane.org/gmane.culture.media.idc/1415.

Davidoff, Leonore. *Worlds Between: Historical Perspectives on Gender and Class.* NY: Routledge, 1995.

De Cew, Judith Wagner. "Privacy." *Stanford Encyclopedia of Philosophy.* 2006. http://plato. stanford.edu/entries/privacy.

Defoe, Daniel. *Robinson Crusoe.* http://www.gutenberg.org/ebooks/521.

Deleuze, Gilles. "Postscript on the Societies of Control." *October* 59, 1992, 3-7.

Descartes, René. *Meditations on First Philosophy*. Princeton UP, 2008.

Deutscher, Isaac. "*1984*–The Mysticism of Cruelty." 29-40. In *Twentieth-century Interpretations of 1984*. Edited by Samuel Hynes. Englewood Cliffs, NJ: Prentice-Hall, Inc., 1971.

Dickens, Charles. *The Pickwick Papers*. NY: Oxford UP, 1987.

Donoghue, Daniel. *Lady Godiva: A Literary History of the Legend*. Malden, MA: Blackwell Publishing, 2003.

Donzelot, Jacques. *L'invention du social: essai sur le déclin des passions politiques*. Paris: Seuil, 1994.

Dostoevsky Fyodor. *Notes From the Underground*. NY: W. W. Norton & Company, 2001.

Doyle, Sir Arthur Conan. *The Complete Sherlock Holmes*. Garden City, NY: Doubleday & Company, Inc., 1930. Volume 1.

Druckrey, Timothy. "Secreted Agents, Security Leaks, Immune Systems, Space Wars . . . " 150-157. In Levin.

Durham, John C. "Durkheim on the Sacred." 2001. http://www.bytrentsacred.co.uk/ index.php/durkheim-on-religion/durkheim-on-the-sacred.

Durkheim, Émile. "The Determination of Moral Facts." 1906. 16-31. In *Sociology and Philosophy*. NY: Routledge, 2010.

Edwards, Justin D. *Exotic Journeys: Exploring the Erotics of U. S. Travel Literature. 1840-1930*. Hanover, NH: University Press of New England, 2001.

Elias, Norbert. *The Civilizing Process*. NY: Urizen Books, 1978.

Elliott, Anthony. *Concepts of the Self*. Cambridge, UK: Polity, 1991.

Elshtain, Jean Bethke. "Comment on Morris's 'Privacy, Privation, Perversity: Toward New Representations of the Personal.'" *Signs* 25(2), 2000, 360-363.

Emerson, Ralph Waldo. *English Traits. Collected Works*. Cambridge: Harvard UP, 1994. Volume 5.

________. "Self-Reliance." 145-169. *The Complete Essays . . .* NY: Modern Library, 1950.

Erasmus. *In Praise of Folly*. http://www.gutenberg.org/ebooks/30201.

Etzioni, Amitai. *Limits of Privacy*. NY: Basic Books, 1999.

"Family Secrets." *Wikipedia*. http://en.wikipedia.org/wiki/Family_secret.

Felluga, Dino. "Modules on Lacan: On the Gaze." *Introductory Guide to Critical Theory*. <http://www.purdue.edu/guidetotheory/psychoanalysis/lacangaze.html>.

Fennetaux, Ariane. "Women 's Pockets and the Construction of Privacy in the Long Eighteenth Century." *Eighteenth-Century Fiction* 20(3), 2008, 307-334.

Fielding, Henry. *Tom Jones*. NY: W. W. Norton & Company, 1995.

Fillingham, Lydia Alix. "'The Colorless Skein of Life': Threats to the Private Sphere in Conan Doyle's *A Study in Scarlet*." *ELH* 56(3), 1989, 667-688.

Foucault. *The Birth of the Clinic: An Archaeology of Medical Perception*. NY: Pantheon, 1977.

________. *Discipline and Punish: The Birth of the Prison.* NY: Vintage Books, 1979.

________. "The Eye of Power." 146-165. *Power/Knowledge: Selected Interviews and Other Writings 1972-1977.* Edited by Colin Gordon. Brighton: Harvester Press, 1980.

Fraser, Nancy. "Foucault on Modern Power: Empirical Insights and Normative Confusions." *Praxis International* 3, 1981, 272-287.

________. *Justice Interruptus: Critical Reflections on the "Postsocialist" Condition.* NY: Routledge, 1997.

________. "Rethinking the Public Sphere: A Contribution to the Critique of Actually Existing Democracy." 1-32. In Robbins.

Frazer. Sir James George. *The Golden Bough: A Study in Magic and Religion.* London: Macmillan and Co., 1924.

Freud. Sigmund. *The Standard Edition of the Complete Psychological Works.* London: 1953-1974, 24 volumes.

Fried, C. *An Anatomy of Values.* Cambridge: Harvard UP, 1970.

Gal, Susan. "A Semiotics of the Public/Private Distinction." 261-277. In Scott and Keates.

Gallagher, Susan E. "A Man's Home: Rethinking the Public/Private Dichotomy in American Political Thought." http://faculty.uml.edu/sgallagher/RPOldconclusion.htm.

Gamson, Joshua. *Freaks Talk Back: Tabloid Talk Shows and Sexual Nonconformity.* University of Chicago Press, 1998.

Gan, Wendy. Women, *Privacy and Modernity in Early Twentieth-century British Writing.* NY: Palgrave Macmillan, 2009.

Garrard, Richard. "Panopticon: Government and Privacy in the New Millenium." 2003. http://www.humanistsofutah.org/2003/Panopticon_Jan-03.html.

Gay, Peter. *The Bourgeois Experience: Victoria to Freud.* NY: Oxford UP, 1984. Volume 1.

Gaylin, Ann. *Eavesdropping in the Novel from Austen to Proust.* NY: Cambridge UP, 2002.

Gerstein, Robert S. "Intimacy and Privacy." *Ethics* 89, 1978, 76-81.

Giddens, Anthony. *Modernity and Self-Identity: Self and Society in the Late Modern Age.* Cambridge, UK: Polity Press, 1991.

Gilbert, Susan and Sandra Gubar. *The Madwoman in the Attic: The Woman Writer and the Nineteenth-century Literary Imagination.* New Haven: Yale UP, 1979.

Giridaran, Vaishnavi. "*We.*" http://mslinder.wikispaces.com/We.

Glancy, Dorothy J. "At the Intersection of Visible and Invisible Worlds: United States Privacy Law and the Internet." *Santa Clara Computer and High Technology Law Journal* 357, 2000, 1-25.

Godwin, William. *Caleb Williams.* Peterborough, ON: Broadview Press, 2000.

Goffman, Erving. *The Presentation of Self in Everyday Life.* University of Edinburgh, 1958.

Goodall, Peter. "Theorizing the Private Sphere." *Cultural Studies Review* 2005 11(2), 30-43.

Goodman, Dena. "Public Sphere and Private Life: Toward a Synthesis of Current Historiographical Approaches to the Old Regime." *History and Theory* 31(1), 1992, 1-20.

Gosseries, Axel. "Publicity." *Stanford Encyclopedia of Philosophy*. http://plato.stanford.edu/entries/publicity/.

Greve, Anni. *Sanctuaries of the City: Lessons From Tokyo*. Burlington, VT: Ashgate, 2011.

Gurstein, Rochelle. *The Repeal of Reticence*. NY: Hill and Wang, 1996.

Habermas, Jürgen. *The Structural Transformation of the Public Sphere*. Cambridge, MA: MIT Press, 1989.

Harding, Anthony John. "'Domestick Privacies': Biography and the Sanctifying of Privacy, from Johnson to Martineau." *Dalhousie Review* 85(3), 2005, 371-389.

Harper, David. "The Politics of Paranoia: Paranoid Positioning and Conspiratorial Narratives in the Surveillance Society." *Surveillance & Society* 5(1), 2008, 1-32.

Hart. Francis R. "The Spaces of Privacy: Jane Austen." *Nineteenth-century Fiction* 30(3), 1975, 305-333.

Hawthorne, Nathaniel. *Novels*. NY: The Library of America, 1983.

________. *Tales*. 1982.

Heinämaa, Sara and Martina Reuter. *Psychology and Philosophy: Inquiries Into the Soul from Late Scholasticism*. Dordrecht: Springer, 2009.

Hobbes, Thomas. *Leviathan, or, the Matter, Form, and Power of a Commonwealth*. Yale UP, 2010.

Hollander. John. "Private/Public: The Evolution of the Distinction." *Social Research* 68(1), 2001, 5-28.

Holm, Nicholas. "Conspiracy Theorizing Surveillance: Considering Modalities of Paranoia and Conspiracy in Surveillance Studies." *Surveillance Studies* 7(1), 2009, 36-48.

Hoy, David Couzens. "Power, Repression, Progress: Foucault, Lukes and the Frankfurt School." 123-148. In *Foucault: A Critical Reader*. Edited by Hoy. NY: B. Blackwell, 1986.

Hugo, Victor. *Les Misérables*. NY: Alfred A. Knopf, 1997.

Hulme, Peter. *Colonial Encounters: Europe and the Native Caribbean, 1492-1797*. NY: Routledge, 1992.

Hunt, Aeron. "Open Accounts: Harriet Martineau and the Problem of Privacy in Early-Victorian Culture." *Nineteenth-Century Literature* 62(1), 2007, 1-28.

Irving, Washington. "The Stout Gentleman." 49-56. *Bracebridge Hall, or, The Humourists*. Boston: Twayne Publishers, 1977.

Jagodzinski, Cecile M. *Privacy and Print: Reading and Writing in Seventeenth-century England*. Charlottesville: University Press of Virginia, 1999.

James, Henry. *Complete Notebooks*. Edited by Leon Edel and Lyall H. Powers. NY: Oxford UP, 1987.

________. *Novels 1881-1886* . . . NY: The Library of America, 1985.

________. *Novels 1886-1890* . . . 1989.

________. *The Reverberator*. London: Rupert Hart-Davis, 1949.

James, William. *The Principles of Psychology*. NY: H. Holt and Company, 1905. Volume 2.

Jay, Martin. *Downcast Eyes: The Denigration of Vision in Twentieth-century French Thought*. Berkeley: University of California Press, 1994.

Johnson, Gerald. "The Invasion of Privacy (4): Laus Contemptionis." *American Scholar* 28(4), 1959, 447-457.

Johnson, Paul Christopher. *Secrets, Gossip, and Gods: the Transformation of Brazilian Candomblé*. NY: Oxford UP, 2002.

Johnson, Pauline. *Habermas: Rescuing the Public Sphere*. NY: Routledge, 2006.

Kant, Immanuel. *Toward Perpetual Peace and Other Writings on Politics, Peace, and History*. New Haven: Yale UP, 2006.

Kateb, George. "On Being Watched and Known." *Social Research* 68(1), 2001, 269-295.

Keane, John. "Public Life in the Era of Communicative Abundance." *Canadian Journal of Communication* 24(2), 1999, 165-178.

Keenan, Thomas. "Windows of Vulnerability." 121-141. In Robbins.

Kelly, Dorothy. *Telling Glances: Voyeurism in the French Novel*. New Brunswick, NJ: Rutgers UP, 1992.

Kent, Jr., Michael B. "Pavesich, Property and Privacy: The Common Origins of Property Rights and Privacy Rights in Georgia." *John Marshall Law Journal* 2, 2009, 1-22.

Klimasmith Betsy. *At Home in the City: Urban Domesticity in American Literature and Culture, 1850–1930*. Hanover: University Press of New England, 2005.

Koch, Mark. "Ruling the World: The Cartographic Gaze in Elizabethan Accounts of the New World." *Early Modern Literary Studies* 4(2), 1998. http://extra.shu.ac.uk/emls/04-2/kochruli.htm.

Koskela, Hille. "Video surveillance, gender, and the safety of public urban space: 'Peeping Tom' goes high tech?" *Urban Geography* 23(3), 2002, 257-278.

Krips, Henry. "The Politics of the Gaze: Foucault, Lacan and Žižek." *Culture Unbound*. 2, 2010: 91–102.

Kundera, Milan. *The Unbearable Lightness of Being*. NY: Harper & Row, 1984.

Lacoste, Guillermine De . "Sartre's 'new gaze' in *Saint Genet*: a Lacanian reading." *Sartre Studies International* 10.1, 2004, 44-60.

Lamb, Charles. *The Letters of Charles and Mary Anne Lamb*. Edited by Edwin W. Marrs, Jr. Ithaca: Cornell UP, 1975.

Lasch, Christopher. *The Culture of Narcissism: American Life in an Age of Diminishing Expectations*. NY: Warner Books, 1971.

Leap, William, editor. *Public Sex/Gay Space*. NY: Columbia UP, 1999.

Lester, Toby. "The Reinvention of Privacy." *The Atlantic Monthly* 287(3), 2001, 27-39.

Levin, Thomas, Ursula Frohne and Peter Weibel, editors. *CTRL [SPACE]: Rhetorics of Surveillance from Bentham to Big Brother*. Cambridge: MIT Press, 2002.

Locke. Thomas. *An Essay Concerning Human Understanding*. Oxford: Clarendon Press, 1975.

________. *The Second Treatise of Government*. NY: Bobbs-Merrill Company, Inc., 1952.

Lucian of Samosata. "Hermotimus." *Selected Dialogues*. NY: Oxford UP, 2005.`

Lupton, Deborah. "Foucault and the Medicalisation Critique." 20-24. In *Death and Dying*. Edited by Sarah Earle, Carol Komaromy, and Caroline Bartholomew. LA: Sage, 2009.

Lyon, David. *The Electronic Eye: The Rise of the Surveillance Society*. Cambridge: Polity Press, 1994.

Lyu, Claire. "Unswathing the Mummy: Body, Knowledge, and Writing in Gautier's Le *Roman de la momie*." *Nineteenth-Century French Studies* 33(3 & 4), 2005, 308-319.

McKinnon, Catherine A. *Toward a Feminist Theory of the State*. Cambridge: Harvard UP, 1989.

Marcus, Sharon. "Placing Rosemary's Baby." *differences* 5(3), 1993, 121-153.

Margolis, Eric. "Blind Spots: Thoughts for Visual Sociology Upon Reading Martin Jay's *Downcast Eyes: The Denigration of Vision in Twentieth-Century French Thought*." http://margolis.faculty.asu.edu/review.html.

Margalit, Avishai. "Privacy in the Decent Society." *Social Research* 68(1), 2001, 255-268.

Martin, Robert K, *Hero, Captain, and Stranger: Male Friendship, Social Critique and Literary Form in the Sea Novels of Herman Melville*. Chapel Hill: University of North Carolina Press, 1986.

Matsuda, Matt K. *The Memory of the Modern*. NY: Oxford UP, 1996.

Mattis, Ann. "Vulgar Strangers in the Home": Charlotte Perkins Gilman and Modern Servitude." *Women's Studies* 39(4), 2010, 283–303.

Maturin, Charles Robert. *Melmoth the Wanderer*. http://gutenberg.net.au/ebooks07/0700551h.html.

McDougall, Bonnie. "Privacy--The Psychological Functions And Philosophical Values Of Privacy." http://science.jrank.org/pages/10854/Privacy-Psychological- Functions-Philosophical-Values-Privacy.html.

McGrath, John E. *Loving Big Brother: Performance, Privacy and Surveillance Space*. NY: Routledge, 2004.

McKeon, Michael. *The Secret History of Domesticity*. Baltimore: The Johns Hopkins UP, 2005.

McLaren, Leah. "Turning a Year Older With the Timeless Spalding Gray." *The Globe and Mail*, Nov. 4, 2011. http://www.theglobeandmail.com/news/arts/ leah-mclaren/turning-a-year-older-with-the-timeless-spalding-gray/article2225735/print/.

Melville, Herman. *Pierre . . . Israel Potter . . .* NY: The Library of America, 1984.

________. *Redburn . . . White-Jacket . . . Moby-Dick*. 1983.

Merritt, . "Spying, Writing, Authority: Eliza Haywood's *Bath Intrigues*." *Studies in Eighteenth-century Culture* 30, 2001, 183-99.

Metz, Christian. *Psychoanalysis and Cinema: The Imaginary Signifier*. London: The Macmillan Press Ltd., 1982..

Michaelsen, Scott. "Is Nothing Secret?" *Discourse*, 27(2&3), 2005, 124-154.

Mill, John Stuart. *On Liberty and the Subjection of Women*. NY: Penguin, 2006.

Miller, D. A. *The Novel and the Police*. Berkeley: University of California Press, 1988.

Miller, Nancy K. "Women's Secrets and the Novel." *Social Research* 68(1), 2001, 173-99.

Milton, John. *Samson Agonistes*. 153-204. *Selected Poetry and Prose*. NY: W. W. Norton & Company, 2011.

Mohr, Richard D. "Parks, Privacy and the Police." 1999. http://www.qrd.org/qrd/media/ print/richard.mohr/ 1996/parks.privacy.and.the.police-01.96.

Montaigne, Michel de. *The Complete Works*. Stanford UP, 1943.

Moore, Adam D. "Intangible Property: Privacy, Power, and Information Control." *American Philosophical Quarterly* 35(4), 1998, 365-378.

Moore, Barrington Jr. Privacy: Studies in Social and Cultural History. Armonk, NY: E. Sharpe, 1983.

Mulvey, Laura. "Visual Pleasure and Narrative Cinema". *Screen* 16(3), 1975, 6–18.

Nagel, Thomas. "Concealment and Exposure." *Philosophy & Public Affairs* 27(1), 1998, 3-30.

Nelson, Deborah. *Pursuing Privacy in Cold War America*. NY: Columbia UP, 2002.

Nikolchina, Miglena. "The Seminar: iMode *d'emploi, Impure* Spaces in the Light of Late Totalitarianism." 359-388. In Scott and Keates.

Nock, Steven L. *The Costs of Privacy: Surveillance and Reputation in America*. NY: Aldine de Gruyter, 1993.

Olmstead v. United States - 277 U.S. 438 (1928). http://supreme.justia.com/cases/federal/us/277/438/case.html.

Orlin, Lena Cowen. *Locating Privacy in Tudor London*. NY: Oxford UP, 2007.

Orwell, George. *1984*. London: Secker & Warburg, 1987.

Parenti, Christian. *The Soft Cage: Surveillance in America from Slavery to the War on Terror*. NY: Basic Books, 2003.

Pearson, Maeve. "Re-exposing the Jamesian Child: The Paradox of Children's Privacy." *The Henry James Review* 28(2), 2007, 101-119.

Pecora, Vincent P. "The Culture of Surveillance." *Qualitative Sociology* 25(3), 2002, 345-358.

Pellow. Deborah. "Chinese Privacy." 31-46. In *The Cultural Meaning of Urban Space*. Edited by Richard Rotenberg and Gary McDonogh. London: Bergin & Garvey, 1993.

Phillips, Sandra S. "Looking Out, Looking In: Voyeurism and Its Affinities from the Beginning of Photography." 11-204. In *Exposed: Voyeurism, Surveillance, and the Camera Since 1870*. Edited by Phillips. San Francisco Museum of Modern Art, 2010.

Phillips, James "Life in Space: William Burroughs and the Limits of the Society of Control." *Literature & Aesthetics* 16(1), 2006, 95-112.

Poe, Edgar Allan. a. *Essays and Reviews*. NY: Library of America, 1984.

________. b. *Poetry and Tales*. 1984.

Poole, Adrian. "Henry James and the Mobile Phone." *The Cambridge Quarterly* 37(1), 2008, 79-89.

Porter, Roy. *Rewriting the Self: Histories from the Renaissance to the Present*. NY: Routledge, 1997.

Poster, Mark. *The Second Media Age*. Cambridge, UK: Polity Press, 1995.

Powell, Jim.. "Benjamin Constant: Liberty and Private Life." *The Freeman* 47(10), 1997.

Pratt, May Louise. *Imperial Eyes: Travel Writing and Transculturation.* NY: Routledge, 2008.

Proust, Marcel. *Swann's Way*. 3-330. *Remembrance of Things Past*. NY: Random House, 1934.

"Public Opinion." *Wikipedia*. http://en.wikipedia.org/wiki/Public_opinion.

Rachels, J. "Why Privacy is Important," *Philosophy and Public Affairs* 4, 1975, 323-33.

Renza, Louis A. *Edgar Allan Poe, Wallace Stevens, and the Poetics of American Privacy*. Baton Rouge: Louisiana State UP, 2002.

Riley, Denise. *"Am I That Name?": Feminism and the Category of Women in History*. Minneapolis: University of Minnesota Press, 1988.

________. *The Words of Selves: Identification, Solidarity, Irony*. Stanford UP, 2000.

Robbins, Bruce, editor. *The Phantom Public Sphere*. Minneapolis: University of Minnesota Press, 1993.

Roberts, Lucy. "The history of video surveillance--from VCR's to eyes in the sky." 2005. http://www.articleexposure.net/article153978.html.

Robertson, Roland. "Open Societies, Closed Minds? Exploring the Ubiquity of Suspicion and Voyeurism." *Globalizations* 4 (3), 2007, 399–416.

Rooney, Ellen. "A Semiprivate Room." 333-358. In Scott and Keates.

Rose, Nikolas. "Assembling the Modern Self." 224-248. In Porter.

Rosenbloom, Stephanie. "I Spy; Doesn't Everyone?" *New York Times* Sept. 7, 2006.

http://query.nytimes.com/gst/fullpage.html?res=9806EFD81631F934A357 5AC0A9609C8B63&pagewanted=all.

Ross. *No Respect: Intellectuals & Popular Culture*. NY: Routledge, 1989.

Rössler, Beate. *Privacies: Philosophical Evaluations*. Stanford UP, 2004.

________. *The Value of Privacy*. Cambridge, UK: Polity Press, 2005.

Rossman Neil. *Consciousness: Separation and Integration*. Albany, SUNY Press, 1991.

Rowe, George. "Privacy, Vision, and Gender in Spenser's Legend of Courtesy." *MLQ* 50(4), 1989, 309-336.

Rump: or an exact collection of the choycest poems and songs relating to the late times. In *Censorship and Interpretation: The Condition of Writing and Reading Early Modern England*. Edited by Annabel Patterson. Madison: University of Wisconsin Press, 1984.

Sabin, Margery. "Modern Variations on the Theme of Privacy: Language and the Private Self." 287-304. In *Imagining Selves*. Edited by Rivka Swenson.and Elise Lauterbach. Newark: University of Delaware Press, 2008.

Sanborn, Geoffrey. "Keeping Her Distance: Cisneros, Dickinson, and the Politics of Private Enjoyment." *PMLA* 116(5), 2001, 1334-1348.

Schmitt, Frederick F. and Reza Lahroodi. "The Epistemic Value of Curiosity." *Educational Theory* 58(2), 2008, 125–148.

Schneider, Carl D. *Shame, Exposure and Privacy*. Boston: Beacon Press, 1977.

Schoeman, Ferdinand David. *Philosophical Dimensions of Privacy*. NY: Cambridge UP, 1984.

Schwartz, Barry. "The Social Psychology of Privacy." *The American Journal of Sociology* 73(6), 1968, 741-752.

Scott, Joan W. and Debra Keates. *Going Public: Feminism and the Shifting Boundaries of the Public Sphere*. Urbana: University of Illinois Press, 2004.

Seltzer, Mark. *Henry James and the Art of Power*. Ithaca: Cornell UP, 1984.

Sennett, Richard. *The Fall of Public Man*. NY: Alfred A. Knopf, 1977.

Serres, Michel. "Panoptic Theory." 25-50. In *The Limits of Theory*. Edited by Thomas M. Kavanagh. Stanford UP, 1989.

Shamir, Milette Shamir. "Hawthorne's Romance and the Right to Privacy." *American Quarterly* 49(4), 1997, 746-779.

________. *Inexpressible Privacy: The Interior Life of Antebellum American Literature*. University of Pennsylvania Press, 2006.

Shapiro, Johanna. "(Re)examining the clinical gaze through the prism of literature." *Families, Systems, & Health* 20(2), 2002,161-170.

Sharp, Joanne P. "A Feminist Engagement with National Identity." 94-108. In *Body Space: Destabilizing Geographies of Gender and Sexuality*. Edited by Nancy Duncan. NY: Routledge, 1996.

Shawver, Lois. "Section by Section Paraphrase of Postscript on the Societies of Control. 2006. http://www.douban.com/group/topic/1175489/.

Shelley, Mary. *Frankenstein; or, The Modern Prometheus*. http://www.gutenberg.org/files/84/84-h/84-h.htm.

Simmel, Georg. "Sociology of the Senses: Visual Interaction." 356-360. In *Introduction to the Science of Sociology*. Edited by Robert E. Park and Ernest W. Burgess. University of Chicago Press, 1969.

Smith, Janna Malamud. "Post 9/11 Collision of Privacy and Security." *The Christian Science Monitor* March 22, 2004. http://www.csmonitor.com/2004/0322/p09s01-coop.html

Smith, Robert Ellis. *Ben Franklin's Web Site: Privacy and Curiosity from Plymouth Rock to the Internet*. Providence RI: Privacy Journal, 2000.

Snaith, Anna. *Virginia Woolf: Public and Private Negotiations*. NY: St. Martin's Press, Inc., 2000.

Spacks, Patricia Meyer. *Privacy: Concealing the Eighteenth-century Self.* University of Chicago Press, 2003.

________. "The Privacy of the Novel." *Novel: A Forum on Fiction* 31(3), 1998, 304-316.

Stallybrass, Peter and Allon White. *The Politics and Poetics of Transgression.* London: Methuen, 1968.

Stam, Robert and Roberta Pearson. "Hitchcock's *Rear Window*: Reflexivity and the Critique of Voyeurism." 193-206. In *A Hitchcock Reader*. Edited by Marshall Deutelbaum and Leland Pogue. Ames: Iowa State UP, 1986..

Sterne, Laurence. *Tristram Shandy*. NY: W. W. Norton & Company, 1980.

Stevenson, Robert Louis and Fanny Van de Grift Stevenson. *The Dynamiter*. http://www.gutenberg.org/ebooks/647.

Stoddart, Judith. "Cultures of Print: Mass Markets and Theories of the Liberal Public Sphere." 171-185. In *Authorship, Commerce and the Public: Scenes of Writing, 1750-1850* . Edited by E. J. Clery, Caroline Franklin and Peter Garside. NY: Palgrave Macmillan, 2002.

Stone, Lawrence. *The Family, Sex and Marriage in England 1500-1800*. NY: Harper Colophon, 1977.

"Surveillance." *Wikipedia*. http://en.wikipedia.org/wiki/Surveillance.

Sykes, Charles J. *The End of Privacy*. NY: St. Martin's Press, 1999.

________. "Invasion of the Privacy Snatchers." *Hoover Digest* 4, 2000. http://www.hoover.org/publications/hoover-digest/article/6836.

Szabados, Béla and Eldon Soifer. *Hypocrisy: Ethical Investigations*. Peterborough, ON: Broadview Press, 2004.

Taipale, K. A. "Technology, Security and Privacy: the Fear of Frankenstein, the Mythology of Privacy and the Lessons of King Ludd." *Yale Journal of Law and Technology* 7(123), 2004, 123-171.

Tanney, Julia. "Gilbert Ryle." *Stanford Encyclopedia of Philosophy*. 2009. http://plato.stanford.edu/entries/ryle/.

Thoreau, Henry, David. *Journal. Writings*. Edited by Bradford Torrey. Boston: The Riverside Press, 1906. Volume 10.

________. *Journal*. Edited by Robert Sattelmeyer, Mark Patterson and William Ross. Princeton UP, 1990. Volume 3.

________. *A Week on the Concord and Merrimac Rivers, Walden; or, Life in the Woods* . . . NY: The Library of America, 1985.

Tourney, G. and Dean J. Plazak. "The Evil Eye in Myth and Schizophrenia." *Psychiatric Quarterly* 28(1-4), 1954, 478-495.

Toulmin, Stephen. "The Inwardness of Mental Life." *Critical Inquiry* 6(1), 1979, 1-16.

Tourney, Garfield. "The Evil Eye in Myth and Schizophrenia." *Psychoanalytic Quarterly* 27, 1954, 478-495.

Trollope, Anthony. *The Way We Live Now*. NY: The Modern Library, 2001.

Turner, John S. "Collapsing the Interior/Exterior Distinction: Surveillance, Spectacle, and Suspense in Popular Cinema." *Wide Angle* 20(4), 1998, 93-123.

Vatulescu, Cristina. *Police Aesthetics: Literature, Film, and the Secret Police of Soviet Times*. Stanford UP, 2010.

Veel, Kristin. "Surveillance Narratives–From Lack to Overload." http://www.inter-disciplinary.net/ci/cyber%20hub/visions/v3/Veel%20paper.pdf.

Velecky, Lubor C. "The Concept of Privacy." 13-34. In Young.

Villa, Dana. *Public Freedom*. Princeton UP, 2008.

Wacker, Watts and Jim Taylor. *The 500-year Delta: What Happens After What Comes Next*. NY: HarperBusiness, 1997.

Walker, John A. "Looks, the gaze and surveillance." In *Visual Culture*. Edited by Walker and Sarah Chaplin. Manchester UP, 1997.

Warren, Samuel D. and Louis D. Brandeis. "The Right to Privacy." *Harvard Law Review* 4(5), 1890, 193-220. http://www.gutenberg.org/files/37368/37368-h/37368-h.htm.

Weibel, Peter. "Pleasure and the Panoptic Principle." 206-223. In Levin.

Weintraub, Jeff. "The Theory and Politics of the Public/Private Distinction." 1-42. In *Public and Private in Thought and Practice*. Edited by Weintraub and Krishan Kumar. University of Chicago Press,1997.

Welch, Nancy. "Ain't Nobody's business: a Public Personal History of Privacy after *Baird v. Eisenstadt*." 17-30. In *The Private, the Public and the Published*. Edited by Barbara Couture and Thomas Kent. Logan: Utah State UP, 2004.

Whitaker, Reg. *The End of Privacy: How Total Surveillance is Becoming a Reality*. NY: New Press, 1999.

White, Fred D. "'Sweet skepticism of the heart': Science in the Poetry of Emily Dickinson." *College Literature* 19(1), 1992, 121-129.

Whitman, James. "The Two Western Cultures of Privacy: Dignity versus Liberty." *Yale Law Journal* 113(6), 2004, 1151-1221.

Wordsworth, William. "A Letter to a Friend of Robert Burns." http://www.gutenberg.org/files/16550/16550-h/vol_ii.htm.

________. Selected Poetry. Edited by Stephen Gill and Duncan Wu. NY: Oxford UP, 1997.

Wydeven, Joseph J. "Photography and Privacy: The Protests of Wright Morris and James Agee." *Midwest Quarterly* 23(1), 1981, 103-115 .

Yeazell, Ruth. "Sexuality, Shame and Privacy in the English Novel." *Social Research* 68(1), 119-144.

Young, John B., editor. *Privacy*. NY: John Wiley & Sons, 1978.

Zamyatin, Evgeny. *We*. NY: Modern Library, 2006.

Zbikowski, Dorte. "Bruce Nauman." 64-67. In Levin.

Ziegler, Georgianna. "My lady's chamber: female space, female chastity in Shakespeare." *Textual Practice* 4(1), 1990, 73-100.

Žižek, Slavoj. "Good Manners in the Age of WikiLeaks." *London Review of Books* 33(2), 20 January 2011, 9-10. http://vijana.fm/2011/01/30/ good-manners-in-the-age-of-wikileaks-by-slavoj-zizek/.

INDEX